RELEASED

TELEVISION AND ANTISOCIAL BEHAVIOR

FIELD EXPERIMENTS

ST. JOSEPH'S UNIVERSITY   STX
HE8700.6.M55
Television and antisocial behavior: fiel

3 9353 00159 1104

TELEVISION AND ANTISOCIAL BEHAVIOR

FIELD EXPERIMENTS

STANLEY MILGRAM

R. LANCE SHOTLAND

HE
8700.6
.M55

161653

ACADEMIC PRESS   New York   San Francisco   London   **1973**

A Subsidiary of Harcourt Brace Jovanovich, Publishers

COPYRIGHT © 1973, BY ACADEMIC PRESS, INC.
ALL RIGHTS RESERVED.
NO PART OF THIS PUBLICATION MAY BE REPRODUCED OR
TRANSMITTED IN ANY FORM OR BY ANY MEANS, ELECTRONIC
OR MECHANICAL, INCLUDING PHOTOCOPY, RECORDING, OR ANY
INFORMATION STORAGE AND RETRIEVAL SYSTEM, WITHOUT
PERMISSION IN WRITING FROM THE PUBLISHER.

ACADEMIC PRESS, INC.
111 Fifth Avenue, New York, New York 10003

United Kingdom Edition published by
ACADEMIC PRESS, INC. (LONDON) LTD.
24/28 Oval Road, London NW1

Library of Congress Cataloging in Publication Data

Milgram, Stanley.
　　　Television and antisocial behavior.

　　　Bibliography: p.
　　　1.　Television—Social aspects.　　2.　Deviant
behavior.　　I.　Shotland, R. Lance, joint author.
II.　Title.　[DNLM:　1.　Psychology, Social.
2.　Social behavior.　3.　Television.　HE8700.8
M644t 1973]
HE8700.6.M55　　　　301.16′2　　　　72-12193
ISBN 0-12-496350-1

PRINTED IN THE UNITED STATES OF AMERICA

CONTENTS

PREFACE

For a period of several years we have been engaged in a program of research on a troubling social question: does the depiction of antisocial behavior on television stimulate imitation in the larger community? To carry out this research, a television program was specifically written for the purpose of this study and aired on network television. To assess the effects of the program, our research was carried out in New York, St. Louis, Detroit, and Chicago.

The study had its origins in a meeting of social scientists called by the Office of Social Research at the Columbia Broadcasting System. The director of that office, Dr. Joseph Klapper, had invited social scientists, including the senior author, to discuss the existing studies of television violence and also to devise new ways to study the problem. It seemed clear that existing research lacked a compelling quality. And it did so for a simple reason: Only experiments produce conclusive results, and you cannot have a plausible experiment on the effects of television without having control of the independent variable. So long as the social scientist could not control *what* viewers would see, he could not test cause and effect relationships between television and behavior. The degree to which the networks were seriously interested in carrying out television research would be indicated by the cooperation they extended in giving the social scientist some say in television programming. Moreover, it was the responsibility of the networks to allow meaningful research by more intensive cooperation with social science. This study was undertaken with these principles in mind, and in the belief that social science can provide the tools, but requires cooperation from the networks if these important issues are to be examined. We present here the results of our investigation.

The study was undertaken within the framework of a research project organized by the first author at The City University of New York. The second author served as a Research Associate, and upon termination of the project, became Assistant Professor of Psychology at the Pennsylvania State University. Others who contributed to the project are cited in the Acknowledgments and in Appendix I.

S.M.
R.L.S.

ACKNOWLEDGMENTS

I am most grateful to the producers of *Medical Center,* Frank Glicksman and Al C. Ward, to author Don Brinkley, and to Director Vincent Sherman for their invaluable cooperation in the production of the stimulus program; and to Richard C. Daniels of Project Hope for his generous help.

To Herman Staudenmeyer, who gave skillful service in supervising the field laboratories and helping in the statistical analyses, and to Lawrence Sandek, who prepared an early version of the report, I express my deep appreciation.

The research could not have been carried out without the funding and cooperation of CBS, Inc. Special thanks are due to Dr. Joseph T. Klapper, of the CBS Office of Social Research. The most difficult part to the project was to get the stimulus program produced, and it was Dr. Klapper's office that guided matters through the CBS organization, union restrictions, and budgetary maze to see that this was done. His reasoned, intelligent manner and commitment to this research are a model of enlightened cooperation. Of considerable aid also was Mr. Philip Harding, Dr. Klapper's assistant.

The following persons served as research assistants: Ralph Lindsey, Tatsu Oshiro, David Greene, John Sabini and Lynne Goodstein; also Harry From, Samuel Gelbtuch, Daniel Geller, Kathryn Krogh, Maury Silver, Steve Sumii, and Wendy Sternberg. Bill Lyons and Howard Simpson assisted in setting up closed-circuit television for the experiments. Mary Englander, Eileen Lyddall, Alexandra Milgram, and Susan Sidney provided secretarial and administrative assistance. To all these persons appreciation is gratefully acknowledged.

Finally, thanks are due to Gerald Graze, Paul Segall, and Ted Leathem of the Research Foundation of the City of New York for facilitating the execution of a complex research project.

STANLEY MILGRAM,
PRINCIPAL INVESTIGATOR

INTRODUCTION

This is a report of research designed to test whether the content of television programs has a measurable effect on behavior. It aims more specifically, at discovering the extent to which an antisocial act depicted on television stimulates imitation among its viewers. We hope that in addition to its substantive findings the report will contribute to the methods by which such studies are pursued.

Excellent reviews of relevant theory and research have recently appeared (Singer, 1971; Feshbach & Singer, 1971); and though it would be superfluous to deal with them at length, we shall touch on some highlights:

1. The prevalence of violent acts on commercial television in the United States is undisputed. Gerbner (1971), defining violence as the use of physical force against others or one's self, either voluntarily or under compulsion, found that during prime television time in 1968–1969 violent incidents were depicted on the three networks at the rate of eight times an hour.

Barcus (1971), examining Saturday morning childrens' programming, reported that three of ten dramatic segments were "saturated with violence, [and] that 71 percent had at least one instance of human violence with or without the use of weapons . . ."

2. Investigations into the effects of violence have been of two general types: surveys and experimental laboratory studies. In typical laboratory studies, such as that of Bandura, Ross, and Ross (1963), children are exposed to film models of aggressive behavior, and are then observed in their play with toys, such as the Bobo doll.

Hartley (1964), clearly stated the limitation of this type of study:

> When we consider what constituted "aggression" and what behavior was referred to as indicating "violence" in the view of the investigators originally quoted, we are faced with a problem in communication. If a child pummels a toy that is primarily created to be pummeled, or chooses to play with one rather than another mechanical toy, or even bangs his toys about—are these the kinds of "aggressive" acts that cause parental or social concern? Is it valid to bracket these behaviors with the murderous knife-fights of unstable adolescents and to refer to them by the same rubric, as Bandura (1963) and Berkowitz (1962) do, both directly and by implication?

Survey studies, such as that conducted by Himmelweit, Oppenheim, and Vance (1958), go beyond the laboratory in scope. But they suffer from the purely correlational nature of their findings. For example, if known criminals prove to have watched more violence on television than normal persons, we still do not know if exposure to television violence caused their criminal acts, or whether their addiction to television violence reflects a general preoccupation with violence.

3. A study by Feshbach and Singer (1971) broke new ground by introducing more natural circumstances for experimentally testing the effects of television violence. The investigators exposed several groups of boys in a camp to violence-rich or violence-poor television diets over a period of 6 weeks. They then studied the degree of aggressive play among the youngsters and found that the violence-rich group displayed less aggressive behavior in real life than the group exposed to violence-poor television fare.

An additional group of studies, sponsored by the United States Public Health Service (1972), was undertaken after the present research was underway: it did not influence our investigation and so will not be discussed here.

THE PRESENT INQUIRY

Two main principles shape the present inquiry. The first is that we study the effects of television under natural circumstances. This applies both to the viewing situation and to the setting in which the potential influence of the program is assessed. Laboratory studies typically create an aura in which the act of "aggression" loses all socially significant meaning.

The second principle is that logically compelling results can be obtained only by using an experimental design, one in which the investigator varies the value of the suspected cause and notes whether that leads to corresponding variations in the suspected effect. In this investigation, the content of a television program is subjected to controlled variation.

We expose the viewer, under a naturalistic set of circumstances, to a television program depicting antisocial behavior. The viewer is then presented with temptations in real life similar to those faced by the television character. The question is whether the television character's depicted actions influence the real life behavior of the viewers. And, of course, we run a control, a parallel condition featuring a television drama in which antisocial behavior was not an element.

What antisocial act should be used? It must be nontrivial, and hence constitute a meaningful antisocial act by the subject; it must be specific, so that the subject's commission of it can be clearly linked to its television enactment; but it must not be so grave an act that, should it be imitated outside the laboratory, the community would actually suffer serious consequences. And finally, it had to be embedded in a proper dramatic context.

The interplay of these requirements led us to settle upon an act in which the protagonist of a drama destroys a medical-charity collection-box and steals its contents. The act was well suited to our purposes: devoid of personal violence, it yet had real antisocial significance—destruction, theft and, moreover, theft from a beneficent social institution.

The next step was to embed the act in a proper dramatic context. We considered creating a special television program, with new characters, and presenting it as a television "special."[1] But this entailed two major problems: First, it is very hard to generate large audiences for special dramatic programs, and the larger the audience we could obtain for the purpose of our study, the better. Second, we did not wish to alert the audience to the fact that something unusual was afoot; we wanted the antisocial act to appear in as natural a context as possible. These factors convinced us that it would be better to embed the act in an existing television series, which for practical reasons had to be a CBS program.

We rejected such programs as *Mission Impossible* and *Mannix* because they regularly depict such a degree of violence that our experimental act would appear trivial by comparison. We also rejected such a situation comedy as *My Three Sons,* which lacks the serious tone needed for the study.

In the end, we selected *Medical Center*, a typical hospital drama whose many episodes were entirely independent of one another, connected only by Dr. Gannon and a few other abiding characters. It would be feasible to write an episode around our planned incident without affecting the overall series, and the show, rated among the top 15, could deliver the sizable audience our experiment demanded. *Medical Center* seemed optimal for our purposes.

THE SCENARIO

The scenario, created for the purposes of this experiment, was to have at its core the smashing of medical charity boxes.

The program centers around Tom Desmond, a young, white attendant at the Center, a recent father and owner of a small boat, with which he earns some extra money. At the beginning of the program, Tom quits his job, then changes his mind and asks Dr. Gannon to rehire him, but the job is no longer available. Tom's need for money grows desperate; his wife has fallen ill and he has defaulted in payments on the boat.

---

[1]Actually, a special program was written, incorporating the antisocial act. But it was a poor program dramatically, and we deemed it unacceptable for the purposes of the experiment.

Meanwhile, Dr. Gannon, participating in a drive to raise funds for a community clinic, appears on a telethon and informs viewers that collection boxes for the charity have been distributed throughout the city. (The boxes, in fact, have been in evidence at the hospital during the opening sequences of the episode.)

As the critical sequence approaches, we find the dispirited Tom in a bar; one of the collection boxes appears unobtrusively in a corner. The television set is tuned to Gannon, who is asking viewers to call in pledges. Frustrated and angry, Tom dials the telethon but instead of making a pledge he pours abuse into the telephone. He calls in again, and is again abusive. Finally, he picks up a bludgeon, smashes the collection box, pockets the contents, and runs into the street.

An exciting sequence ensues: to a pulsating jazz accompaniment and with quick camera work, Tom roams the streets searching out more collection boxes. He finds one and smashes into it, pockets the money, and runs on to another and another. He finds five in all, and he smashes and pilfers all of them.

There is little question that this antisocial sequence, which occurs in the last quarter of the program, constitutes the dramatic highpoint of the episode.

FOUR STIMULUS PROGRAMS

In order to provide stimulus material for experimental comparisons, the story was written and filmed in three separate versions. Two of the versions use the outline above and differ only in the consequences to Tom. The third version omits the antisocial sequence.

Version 1: Antisocial Behavior with Resulting Punishment(WP)

After Tom smashes the last charity box, he is apprehended by the police and jailed. He learns that it was unnecessary for him to break into the charity banks, for Dr. Gannon was willing to lend him the money needed to retrieve his boat. His marriage also appears to have broken up. This is a conventional ending, in that broadcast code requirements state that crime must not go unpunished.

Version 2: Antisocial Behavior, No Punishment (NP)

After the crime is committed, Tom is chased by the police. But he eventually escapes to Mexico, where his wife will join him. Since the culprit gets away with the crime, this program would not ordinarily be shown on television.

Version 3: Prosocial Behavior (PRO)

In the prosocial version, Tom never breaks into the charity displays, although he seriously considers it, nor does he make any abusive telephone calls. He gets to the point of raising a bludgeon to break the boxes, then he thinks of his wife and child, and refrains from doing so. Finally, he drops a coin into one of the charity displays.

Neutral Story

It is possible, of course, that the mere suggestion of an antisocial act on television is sufficient to provoke its imitation, whether or not the act is actually carried out. For example, a group of TV conspirators might talk about blowing up the Empire State Building without actually doing so, and this could conceivably be sufficient to instill this idea in someone. Therefore, we thought it best to use an unrelated episode of *Medical Center* as part of the experiment. For this purpose, we employed a sequence centering on a love affair between a foreign service officer and his long-suffering lady friend. This episode is romantic, sentimental, and entirely devoid of any violence or antisocial behavior.

Thus, four stimulus programs were used through the course of the experiment:

1. Antisocial behavior with punishment (WP)
2. Antisocial behavior with no punishment (NP)
3. Prosocial program (PRO)
4. Neutral program

Version 1 would test whether the depiction of an antisocial act engenders imitation. But because viewers of that version might be inhibited from imitation because the protagonist was punished, we would test another group with Version 2, in which he is not punished. Version 3 would indicate whether the mere contemplation of an antisocial act might motivate one in the same situation to commit the act, or whether Desmond's restraint and charitable contribution would induce prosocial imitation. And finally, the neutral program would provide a base line: the incidence of antisocial behavior among subjects who had not seen any of the experimental programs.

THE BASIC SCENARIO

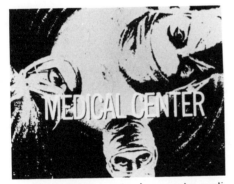

1. The stimulus program is a popular medical series.

2. Tom Desmond (right) works as an attendant at *Medical Center*. Collection banks for a Community Clinic are seen.

3. Tom is scolded by Dr. Joe Gannon for poor work habits, and subsequently loses his job.

4. A *Medical Center* Telethon is held to support the charity drive.

All photos copyright © Metro-Goldwyn-Mayer Inc.

ANTISOCIAL VERSION WITH PUNISHMENT

1. Tom makes an abusive telephone call to the Telethon.

2. Tom on the brink of smashing into the charity bank.

3. The antisocial act.

4. Tom is punished for his action.

All photos copyright © Metro-Goldwyn-Mayer Inc.

ASSESSING THE EFFECTS OF THE
PROGRAM: GENERAL IDEA

The next step in the logic of the design is to assess the effects on viewers of the several versions of the stimulus program. Toward this end, groups which have seen different versions of the program need to be exposed to an authentic charity display, and a comparison of the destruction rates of the several groups would constitute the principal experimental datum.

THE OTHER STIMULUS PROGRAMS

1. In the Antisocial version without punishment, Tom escapes arrest.

2. His wife receives word that he is safe, and in Mexico, where she will join him.

3. In the Prosocial version, Tom does not break into the charity banks, but contributes money to them.

4. The Neutral Program centers on the love affair of a career diplomat. It is completely devoid of violence.

All photos copyright © Metro-Goldwyn-Mayer Inc.

We recruited our subjects and exposed them to our stimulus program in a preview theater, over the air, or via simulated broadcasts on closed circuit television. And we promised all subjects a prize for their participation—a General Electric transistor radio.

The promise served several functions. It served, first, to attract our audiences. It served also to get our subjects to the laboratory, which in the guise of one or another gift-distribution company, presented our subjects with the opportunity to emulate Desmond's antisocial behavior. And finally, by properly scheduling the dates on which our subjects could pick up their radios, we could assure a smooth flow of traffic, with neither too few nor too many arrivals on any one date.

The gift-distribution center was on the 23rd floor of 130 West 42nd Street, an office building of somewhat faded distinction surrounded by a motley assortment of shops and banks, and pornographic bookstores, and movie houses. It is a busy and informal thoroughfare, where our subjects would feel no necessity to dress up to make an appearance, which meant one less impediment to their participation.

Upon arriving on the 23rd floor, our subject could consult a directory, which directed him to the office of *Bartel World Wide* or one of the five other dummy gift-distribution firms we had set up for the study. The furnishings of all were virtually identical and entirely conventional: draped windows, pictures and advertising posters, a few chairs, a scattering of ashtrays and artificial flowers, a coatrack and telephone, and dominating the room, a formica counter. But no office personnel were to be seen.

Two other elements, critical to our experiment, were in each office: a handwritten note taped to the counter that, in the first experiment, said:

NOTICE

We have no more transistor radios to distribute. This distribution center is closed until further notice.

—wording designed to dash the subject's hope that he would get the prize he was promised. We intended, too, that the brusque notice would suggest that no one was present; that the subject was alone in an office where he had anticipated a pleasant experience rather than the frustrating one he was now undergoing.

It was upon the other critical element of furnishings that the subject could, if he were inclined, imitate Tom Desmond's antisocial behavior: a display mounted on one of the walls bearing a poster that showed a surgeon treating a little girl, a picture of a hospital ship, and the words, "Where There Is Hope There Is Life. Project Hope. A people-to-people program of medical education and treatment for developing nations." And mounted on the display, a clear plastic container with some change, a ten-dollar bill and four singles, one of which (dubbed The Dangling Dollar) stuck slightly out of the container.

This was the focus of our experiment: would the subject emulate the antisocial behavior he had seen in the television drama? Had that experience increased the likelihood of his behaving in a similar way? Concealed television cameras enabled us to watch.

In a few minutes the subject would leave the office and retrace his steps to the door that had admitted him to the corridor, only to find it locked. Arrows direct him to the exit; following them, he finds himself not at the elevators, but in a small room. A clerk appears at a teller's window and politely asks, "Are you here for your radio, sir? Sorry about the inconvenience, but we're distributing the radios here, since the *Bartel* people are ill. Do you have a gift certificate?"

Upon countersigning the certificate (so that we could later check the recipient of the radio had indeed seen the stimulus program), he received his prize neatly boxed, was thanked for coming, and left, his contribution to socio-psychological research at an end.

Experiment I

THE FIRST PREVIEW SCREENING

At the outset, we did not wish to broadcast the stimulus material on regular television channels; we needed to develop and refine our assessment techniques without "wasting" the program on several million viewers. The problem was to expose a sufficient, but not excessive, audience to the program. Our approach was to bring several hundred participants together in a midtown auditorium and show them a version of the stimulus program on film. Then we assessed the effect of the film on their behavior.

RECRUITING THE AUDIENCE

We wanted a large but not unwieldy audience, a cross section of the population with a good proportion of young men and disadvantaged minorities, federal statistics (Uniform Crime Reports, 1970) having shown that most thefts other than shoplifting are committed by those segments of the population.

We used two recruitment methods. In the first, we advertised in the *New York Daily News, The Amsterdam News,* and *El Diario,* the New York Spanish-language daily, asking readers to send in a coupon if they cared to receive a transistor radio in return for giving us their reaction to a TV program they would see.

We also recruited participants from the streets, distributing business reply cards at subway stations in both black and white neighborhoods during rush hours, and at high schools at the end of the school day. The postcard bore the same copy as the newspaper ad except for the addition of a line restricting the participants' age to 16 to 40.

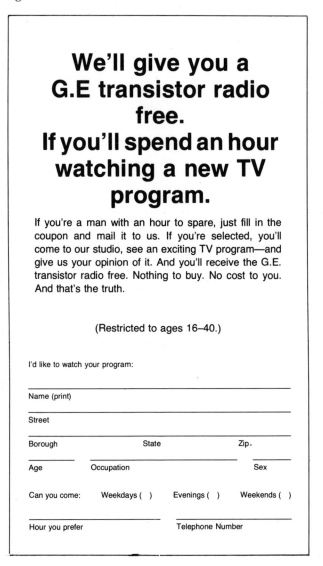

We'll give you a G.E transistor radio free.
If you'll spend an hour watching a new TV program.

If you're a man with an hour to spare, just fill in the coupon and mail it to us. If you're selected, you'll come to our studio, see an exciting TV program—and give us your opinion of it. And you'll receive the G.E. transistor radio free. Nothing to buy. No cost to you. And that's the truth.

(Restricted to ages 16–40.)

I'd like to watch your program:

_____
Name (print)

_____
Street

_____
Borough   State   Zip.

_____
Age   Occupation   Sex

Can you come: Weekdays ( )   Evenings ( )   Weekends ( )

_____
Hour you prefer   Telephone Number

We received 1018 responses, which we divided into four groups (one for each of our experimental programs and the fourth, neutral one), balancing the groups for age and, through random assignment, for other characteristics.

In a few days we sent our respondents invitations on a *Television Previews* letterhead, informing them that they could bring a friend if they wished but that the friend would not be eligible for a prize. And we instructed the four groups to appear at one of four specified screenings (on consecutive Thursdays, at 6 and 8 p.m.) at the Network Television Preview Theater. (This theater had, in fact, been used to gauge audience reaction to TV programs and commercials for marketing and advertising concerns for several years; we could capitalize on the theater's authenticity to enhance our credibility.)

Of the 1018 persons who were sent invitations, a total of 607, consituting groups of between 137 and 162, actually reported to the theater.

PRESENTATION OF STIMULUS PROGRAMS

At the Network Television Preview Theater, participants found a comfortable auditorium, manned by a staff of professional ushers, who collected their letters of invitation, led them to their seats, and distributed questionnaires and writing instruments. Five minutes after the scheduled hour, a master of ceremonies welcomed the participants, and discussed the need that people in television have for the opinions of viewers. He informed the subjects they would see a preview of *Medical Center*, and that we would be interested in their opinions of the program. Participants filled out some preliminary questions on age, sex, and television viewing habits. Then, the lights dimmed, and subjects were exposed to a one-hour episode of the stimulus program, projected in color on the theater's professional-size movie screen. No commercials were shown.

After the screening, the emcee led the audience through the rest of the questionnaire, reading the questions and pausing while they wrote their answers, turning at last to the gift certificate, which they were to sign. He then instructed the audience to take their certificates to *Bartel World Wide* or one of the other companies specified on the certificate, at the time also specified there (M, Tu, W, F 11–7; Sat 9–5), where, he said, they would countersign and surrender the certificates in exchange for their radios. Subjects were then thanked for coming and dismissed.

The gift certificate procedure enabled us to solve a major technical problem: we had to assess the behavior of several hundred subjects at the gift-distribution center, but we could not have them all arrive simultaneously, for we wanted them exposed individually to the charity display. It would not be realistic to schedule each subject for a specific hour and minute to pick up the transistor radio. The solution was to stagger the pick-up dates over a one-week period, and also over six gift companies. In this way we hoped to keep subject collisions to an acceptable level. To minimize effects idiosyncratic to any of the six laboratory testing rooms, half of each audience was directed to a different testing room on different days.

SUBJECTS

Three-hundred and forty-two, or 70% of those who received gift certificates came to the laboratory for their radios. Fifty-three of these subjects were eliminated from our analysis because they were interrupted just before or during the test by other arrivals, encounters which we felt might have affected the spontaneity of their behavior.[1] Of the remaining 289 subjects, 89% were male, 12% had not completed high school, 14% had completed graduate or professional schools, 17% were between 15 and 19, 14% were over 50, 25% were nonwhite. (See Table 11, pages 58–59).

ASSESSMENT PROCEDURE

From the time the subject reached the 23rd floor and stepped off the elevator to the time he left, he was observed via concealed

---

[1] Inclusion of these "excluded" subjects in the analysis of results does not alter the outcome of any experiment reported in this book.

CODING SHEET

TELEVISION PROJECT

Experimental series _____ Subject # _____ Room _____

Treatment condition _____ Date _____ Loc:

Investigator coding behavior _____ Time _____

Brief description Male White Age Estimate _____
of subject: Female Black Other _____

PRELIMINARY   Check box only if
specific behavior occurs

1. Room is empty at time subject enters. (if not, specify) ( )

2. Subject enters alone (i.e. not accompanied by others,
   whether he knows them or not.) If accompanied,
   specify. ( )

3. Subject reads sign indicating no radios to be distributed
   (indicate reactions, if any). ( )

4. Subject appears to notice, look at, or study donation
   box. ( )

PRO-SOCIAL SEQUENCE

5. Takes money from pocket or wallet as if he were about
   to donate it to box. ( )

6. Donates money. ( )* Specify amount.

ANTI-SOCIAL SEQUENCE

7. Handles donation box without placing money in it.　　( )

8. Picks up instrument that could be used to damage or detach donation box.　　( )

9. Attempts to pry donation box open, or free from mounting, or attempts to pry mounting from wall.　　( )

10. Attempts to smash donation box.　　( )*

11. Takes the money or entire donation box.　　( )*

12. Damages or steals other items in room.　　( )

13. Enters more than one room (code behavior on additional coding sheet, attach to this one).　　( )

NEUTRAL BEHAVIOR SEQUENCE

14. Leaves room without any of above anti-social or pro-social actions.　　( )*

15. Subject interrupted in room by entry of another person (specify at what point in sequence).　　( )*

16. Subject surrenders gift certificate (if not, why not).　　( ) Certificate Number:

Did certificate number agree with treatment condition inferred from room or date: Yes　　No　　S's Name _____

Comments, anomalies

Full or emergency scoring (circle one)
* = abridged emergency coding.

television cameras. Working at monitors in the control room, we coded descriptions of the subject and his behavior. We noted whether the premium office was empty when he entered it and whether he entered alone; whether he stole from the collection box or donated to it; whether he took other items from the office, or whether his behavior was entirely neutral. (The coding sheet is shown on pages 16 and 17.)

Additionally, fractional behavior that could lead to antisocial or prosocial behavior was noted. Thus, we noted whether the subject attempted to pry open the donation box, and whether or not he was successful in doing so. These fractional behaviors were coded because the stimulus material may lead to the initiation of an antisocial act that is not consummated. Moreover, we considered this detail pertinent to our study because an unfulfilled antisocial action is, before the law, nonetheless culpable; witness such legally defined crimes as *attempted* murder, *attempted* robbery, and so on.

Upon entering any of the unoccupied offices, our subjects looked about and discovered the notice taped to the counter. Their reaction was typically one of annoyance: they would pace the room, walk behind the counter, sometimes scrawl obscenities on the notice. Subjects invariably focused their attention on the charity display, with its pictures of the surgeon and child, the medical ship, and the attached collection box. This was the critical juncture. In nearly all cases, the subject left the room within a minute or two of his arrival.

RESULTS

Before examining the effects of specific viewing conditions, we need to ask whether any antisocial behavior occurred at all, irrespective of viewing condition. For the total absence of such behavior in any subjects would indicate that there was really no temptation present, or that there were features of the testing situation that completely inhibited antisocial action. Table 1 shows that this is not the case.

The fact that subjects engage in some antisocial action establishes the technical adequacy of the assessment situation, but it does not

TABLE 1

Proportion of Subjects Performing Antisocial Acts in Experiment I (All Versions of Program)[a]

Broke into bank and stole money	5.2%	(15)
Removed Dangling Dollar only	3.5%	(10)
Unsuccessfully attempted to break into bank	6.9%	(20)
Stole other items from room	10.7%	(31)

$N = 289$

[a]The first four categories of antisocial behavior are not mutually exclusive. A single individual would have been scored for three acts if (*a*) he unsuccessfully attempts to break into bank, (*b*) removes the Dangling Dollar, and (*c*) steals other items from the room. A final convention: If a subject breaks into the charity bank and steals the money, he was scored for the first category (broke into bank and stole money), but was not scored for the second category (removed Dangling Dollar only), since in breaking into the bank, the Dangling Dollar became part of the general loot. The percentages reported in the tables are the percentage of subjects performing each specific antisocial act. This system is employed throughout, unless otherwise specified.

yet address the main experimental question: what is the effect of different viewing conditions on the rate of antisocial behavior? The results are shown in Table 2.

The three experimental programs (prosocial, antisocial with punishment, antisocial without punishment) do not differ among themselves by any statistical test in the breakage or theft rates they produced. However, the breakage rate in the neutral program (2.8%) appears lower than that produced in the antisocial WP condition (8.5%), though this trend does not reach statistical significance (*p* = .14, one tailed.) Yet, it is the lowest breakage rate of any of the four programs, so perhaps the depiction of Tom Desmond's antisocial act did influence behavior. But the numbers are small, and the finding inconclusive; we need replication to strengthen the case.

TABLE 2

Proportion of Subjects Performing Antisocial Acts According to Stimulus Program in Experiment I

Stimulus Programs

	Neutral (n = 72)		Prosocial (n = 67)		Antisocial WP (n = 71)		Antisocial NP (n = 79)		All versions (N = 289)		Significance of difference[a] (df = 3)
Broke into bank and stole money	2.8%	(2)	4.5%	(3)	8.5%	(6)	5.1%	(4)	5.2%	(15)	$\chi^2 = 2.46$, n.s.
Removed Dangling Dollar only	4.2%	(3)	6.0%	(4)	4.2%	(3)	0.0%	(0)	3.5%	(10)	$\chi^2 = 4.33$, n.s.
Unsuccessfully attempted to break into bank	4.2%	(3)	11.9%	(8)	8.5%	(6)	3.8%	(3)	6.9%	(20)	$\chi^2 = 4.92$, n.s.
Stole other items from room	13.9%	(10)	13.4%	(9)	8.5%	(6)	7.6%	(6)	10.7%	(31)	$\chi^2 = 2.46$, n.s.

[a] Two tests of significance were used throughout, chi square and the Fisher exact test. Chi square was used when the expected frequencies per cell were six or greater, with one degree of freedom. All chi square values are corrected for continuity when df is equal to 1.

The Fisher exact test was used when expected frequencies per cell were less than six. The Fisher exact test yields probabilities directly (i.e., significance levels), and the absence of a χ^2 value in our reporting of significance indicates the Fisher exact test was employed. Significance levels are reported up to $p = .30$. Beyond .30, we simply designate n.s. (nonsignificant). All reported significance levels are two tailed, unless otherwise specified.

ASSESSING THE EFFECTS OF THE PROGRAM

1. The Field Laboratory was located in this commercial building.

2. Interior of Lancelot Products, one of the dummy gift companies.

3. Interior of Interfax, another gift company.

4. A participant breaks into the charity bank. (dramatized here).

5. Behavior was observed and coded in the control room.

6. Before departure, each subject receives a gift radio.

THE ANTISOCIAL ACT: TOM SMASHES HIS FIRST OF FIVE DONATION BOXES

All photos copyright © Metro-Goldwyn-Mayer Inc.

THE FRUSTRATION STUDY

with Herman Staudenmayer

Our first experiment yielded some slight evidence that an antisocial drama might engender imitation. We wanted now to strengthen the case and, at least as important, to study the conditions under which imitation obtains. More specifically, we wanted to see if frustration was a necessary condition for imitation of the antisocial act seen in the stimulus program. Or would a program lead to imitation, even without frustrating circumstances?

Second, we were aware of the fact that the reaction to the frustrating note was quite strong, and came to dominate the mood of the participant. Perhaps differences due to the stimulus programs would be brought more sharply into relief without frustration; perhaps, the reaction to frustration was so strong that it masked the effects of some of the treatment conditions.

Third, there is a well-known theory in social-psychology that frustration leads to aggression (Dollard, Doob, Miller, Mowrer & Sears, 1939), yet there have been few tests of this notion in naturalistic circumstances. The experiment would give us insight into the general proposition.

Fourth, we wanted some assurance that our dependent variable—breaking into the collection box—was a responsive variable, one that really moved if acted on by appropriate forces. Perhaps the breakage rate was so inherently stable that no experimental manipulation could alter it. If this were true, we could never show the effect of different stimulus progams. The present experiment, therefore, constitutes a test of the sensitivity of our dependent measure.

RECRUITING THE AUDIENCE

Our earlier procedure—newspaper ads and handbills—was cumbersome and costly, and though it netted us a good cross-section of the New York City populace, it did not yield the sizable audience the study needed. Also, in the first experiment we had concentrated on public high schools, and did not wish to use the same schools again.

Despite the possibility that a shift in recruiting procedure might lead to a shift in our subject population, we changed recruiting tactics, resorting now to direct mail, lists for which are relatively cheap and easily obtained.

We used two lists: people who had made installment purchases, and high school seniors. Teenagers, according to Federal studies (Uniform Crime Report, 1970), constitute a high crime-risk group, which, we reasoned, would be responsive to our stimulus materials. Installment buyers would appear, on the face of it, to need money, and thus seemed potentially susceptible to temptation.

We printed our invitations, as before, on *Television Previews* letterheads: 13,468 letters went out, 30% of them to the high school list, and 7% of the invitees actually appeared at the screening.

PRESENTATION OF STIMULUS PROGRAMS

We followed the procedure of our first experiment except for a single detail. Having encountered a total of only four prosocial acts in that earlier test, we decided to drop the prosocial version from the present experiment and concentrate on the versions most likely to elicit antisocial behavior—the WP and NP versions—and, also, the neutral program.

SUBJECTS

About 75% of our theater audiences reported to the gift center/laboratory and, as before, collisions among the subjects disqualified a substantial number. Our final test population was thus 488. Of those, 82% were male; 70%, white; roughly 23%, over 50; some 20% were white collar or professionals; roughly 22%, blue collar (see Table 11).

HOW FRUSTRATION WAS REDUCED

The point at which frustration was strongly aroused occurred when the participant came to pick up the transistor radio and encountered the terse message in the empty distribution office. And this was the point where frustration could be markedly reduced. The technical problem was to expose the participant to the empty office, while at the same time reducing his disappointment. This was done, quite simply, by substituting a new message for the old, one that was considerably more polite, and which informed him that he was about to receive his transistor radio. The new notice read:

NOTICE

Sorry to inconvenience you, but this office
is temporarily closed because of illness.
Kindly pick up your radio in Room 1800 of
this building, where an office will be
kept open until 7 p.m.
Thank you for your cooperation.
—The Management

RESULTS

The data, presented in Table 3, show that neither antisocial version of our program elicited significantly greater rates of antisocial behavior than did the neutral program; no significantly greater incidence of breakage and theft is associated with the WP version

(3.0%) than with the neutral program (8.2%); nor did the NP version (7.6%) fare better. Our other indices yield similar results; theft of the Dangling Dollar did not occur significantly more often with either the WP or NP group (4.0% and 7.6%) than with the neutral program group (5.9%).

Similarly, thefts of other items by the WP and NP audiences (6.9% and 9.8%) were no greater than by viewers of the neutral program (8.2%). Nor did the WP or NP audiences make significantly more attempts at prying into the collection box than did the neutral program audience (1.0% and 4.4% versus 3.5%).

Thus, we did not replicate the trend of the first experiment and that finding is now in grave doubt. The data also show that the high frustration level we induced does not, in fact, mask other behavioral effects, for when we reduced frustration, we still failed to get effects attributable to differences in the stimulus programs.

But quite aside from the effect of the stimulus programs, the presence of frustration proved to be an extremely powerful determinant of antisocial behavior. We can see this most clearly by comparing the percentage of subjects who committed any antisocial acts in the frustration (18.7%) and no frustration (2.9%) conditions; as shown in Table 4.

Six times as many subjects commit antisocial behavior when frustrated. Moreover, the greater frequency of antisocial behavior holds over all categories, and in each of the three stimulus groups. For example, theft from the bank (breakage plus Dangling Dollar) is 11.9% when subjects are frustrated and 1.9% when subjects are not frustrated ($\chi^2 = 15.56$, $df = 1$, $p < .001$).

Our results show, therefore, that the theft rate is, in principle, a responsive dependent variable. Manipulations of level of frustration substantially boost the theft rate; but our manipulation of stimulus programs in contrast, did not affect the theft rate in any clear-cut way.[1]

[1]In interpreting the meaning of the findings, two factors should be noted. First, the specific type of frustration is one in which the subject feels cheated, in that he does not get the reward he expected and feels he deserves. It is frustration centering on a breach of contract. One may therefore find his stealing items from the store to be somewhat "justified," in that in removing ashtrays, artificial flowers, and pictures from the company office he is "getting his due from them." However, the theft from a national charity can in no way be justified, since the money does not belong to the gift company in question. It has nothing to do with the fact that the company did not come forth with the promised radio. Thus, it is a case of the displaced effect of frustration.

TABLE 3

Proportion of Subjects Performing Antisocial Acts According to Level of Frustration and Stimulus Program

Stimulus Program

	Neutral		Antisocial WP		Antisocial NP		Significance of differences $df = 2$	
	High frus. (n = 85)	Low frus. (n = 85)	High frus. (n = 101)	Low frus. (n = 89)	High frus. (n = 92)	Low frus. (n = 36)	Among high frus. conditions (n = 278)	Among low frus. conditions (n = 210)
Broke into bank and stole money	8.2% (7)	2.4% (2)	3.0% (3)	0 (0)	7.6% (7)	0 (0)	$\chi^2 = 2.76$, n.s.	$\chi^2 = 2.97$, n.s.
Removed Dangling Dollar only	5.9% (5)	2.4% (2)	4.0% (4)	0 (0)	7.6% (7)	0 (0)	$\chi^2 = 1.19$, n.s.	$\chi^2 = 2.97$, n.s.
Unsuccessfully attempted to break into bank	3.5% (3)	1.2% (1)	1.0% (1)	1.1% (1)	4.4% (4)	0 (0)	$\chi^2 = 2.13$, n.s.	$\chi^2 = .42$, n.s.
Stole other items from room	8.2% (7)	1.2% (1)	6.9% (7)	0 (0)	9.8% (9)	0 (0)	$\chi^2 = .52$, n.s.	$\chi^2 = 1.48$, n.s.

27

TABLE 4

Effects of Frustration on Commission of Antisocial Acts^a

Stimulus program	High frustration	n	Low frustration	n	Significance of difference between high and low frustration conditions $df = 1$
Neutral	21.2%	85	5.9%	85	$\chi^2 = 7.24; p < .008$
Antisocial WP	13.9%	101	1.1%	89	$\chi^2 = 8.88, p < .003$
Antisocial NP	21.7%	92	0	36	$\chi^2 = 7.70, p < .006$
All versions	18.7%	278	2.9%	210	$\chi^2 = 27.20, p < .001$

$N = 488$

^{a}Includes any antisocial act: 21.2% indicates that this percentage of the 85 subjects in the High frustration Neutral condition performed an antisocial act.

THE EFFECTS OF A MODEL:
A SMASHED BANK

The first experiment suggested, however weakly, that an antisocial act depicted on television begets imitation. The second experiment showed, strongly, that frustration greatly increases the level of antisocial behavior. But the second experiment failed to corroborate the imitation finding of the first. Perhaps the stimulus material was not, of itself, sufficiently potent to generate an imitative response; and by the time the subject reached the gift-distribution center, 1 to 7 days after he had seen the film, the effect of the stimulus had worn off. Thus, our next step was to embed a reminder of the antisocial act in the testing situation, a booster, that by interacting with the stimulus program, might provide the needed impetus for an antisocial response.

RECRUITING THE AUDIENCE

We turned again to direct mail, eliminating the list of high school seniors, which we had exhausted for Experiment II, and relying solely on the installment-plan-buyer list.

VIEWING CONDITIONS

As before, subjects saw the stimulus program at a theater—New York's *Town Hall.* This time, however, all subjects viewed either the antisocial WP version or the neutral program; we wanted to have a sufficient number of subjects for statistical analysis, and time was a problem because of the fixed schedule of the upcoming televised test. The WP version was preferred to the NP, because the former is the program that would ordinarily be shown on television.

We also used a different episode of *Medical Center* as the neutral program, for two reasons: first, the new episode was to be part of our upcoming televised tests and we wanted to check it out; and second, to ascertain whether the neutral program we had used in the first two experiments had itself produced such strong effects that they obscured those induced by the antisocial version.

SUBJECTS

Our subjects were, again, a heterogeneous group: of the 238, 41% were black; 25%, under 30; 16%, over 60; their educational and occupational backgrounds were diverse. (See Table 11.)

THE MODEL: A SMASHED DISPLAY

When the subject entered the gift-distribution office, everything was as it had been in earlier experiments, with this exception: a smashed March of Dimes charity display rested on the formica counter, looking as if somebody had broken into it and stolen the money it contained. A screwdriver dangled from the broken container, and a few pennies were left amidst the broken plastic. But the Project Hope wall display was untouched. Thus the subject was presented with a model of antisocial action, in the form of a smashed charity box. And he had an opportunity to imitate the model on the untouched Project Hope bank.

Table 5 indicates that the presence of the booster element—the broken March of Dimes display—had no effect. It did not interact

TABLE 5

*Proportion of Subjects Performing Antisocial Acts
In the Modeling Experiments According to Stimulus Program*

	Stimulus Program			
	Antisocial WP		Neutral	
	Model present ($n = 54$)	Model absent ($n = 55$)	Model present ($n = 65$)	Model absent ($n = 64$)
Broke into bank and stole money	5.6% (3)	5.5% (3)	9.2% (6)	4.7% (3)
Removed Dangling Dollar only	13.0% (7)	9.1% (5)	6.2% (4)	4.7% (3)
Unsuccessfully attempted to break into bank	3.7% (2)	1.8% (1)	3.1% (2)	0% (0)
Stole other items from room	5.6% (3)	9.1% (5)	6.2% (4)	7.8% (5)

$N = 238$

with the antisocial program to produce an effect, nor did it increase antisocial behavior in either neutral or experimental groups.

It is to be recalled that in this experiment, we employed a different neutral program than previously. Perhaps, for some unknown reason, our earlier neutral program had yielded high antisocial levels. But even with a new neutral program, we find no difference between the experimental groups.

IMITATION WHILE VIEWING

Modern psychology has very clearly demonstrated that situations control behavior: the immediate situation acts upon the person with singular power; past ones, far less strongly. Indeed, such experiments as those of Asch (1956), Milgram (1965), and Latané and Darley (1970), show that even the slightest change in the immediate situation may induce large behavioral effects.

Perhaps this explains the failure of our present study to demonstrate a clear and positive connection between our stimulus program and the subjects' subsequent behavior. For while subjects view the stimulus material in one situation, the opportunity for emulation occurs in quite another, that is different in time and place. Perhaps the effects of our programs weaken as they become overlaid with intervening experiences.

To study this, we arranged that our subjects could act immediately after seeing the stimulus program; indeed, that they could act even as they watched it. The assessment procedure would be embedded in the very situation in which the subject viewed the television depiction of antisocial action. Moreover, the subject would be alone with the charity display, not for a few minutes, but for a full hour.

SUBJECTS

Two teams recruited our subjects from the streets of New York's Times Square area. Using signs that read, "Free Ticket For A Color

Television Preview" and calling out a similar message, they attracted passersby and handed them admission tickets. They offered no radio or other prize. Our present subject population was very different from those of our earlier experiments. Some were by all appearances homeless vagrants (a few asked if they could sleep in the labs), others seemed to be alcoholics and drug addicts.

ASSESSMENT

This experiment differed from those that had gone before in that both the stimulus programs and the test occurred at the same time. We cleared the labs of their gift-office paraphernalia, retaining the Project Hope display, and installed a 12-inch color television set and a single chair, so situated that the subject could see the display while watching the set. To diminish suspicion, we stocked the collection box with only $4.45 but omitted the Dangling Dollar.

Our procedure differed, too, in the treatment of our subjects. We wished to impress on them that they would be both anonymous and unobserved. To assure them of the latter, the reception room to which the admission ticket directed them was on the 18th floor— five floors away from the 23rd floor labs. A staff member ushered our subject to an upstairs lab, instructed him to fill in the questionnaire when the show was over, place the completed form in a nearby basket, and leave. As the staff man departed, he gave a further token of the subject's imminent privacy: he was, he said, returning downstairs and would not see the subject again.

To impress the subject that he would remain anonymous, the questionnaire did not ask for his name or address. And to further allay his suspicions, some completed dummy questionnaires were to be seen in the basket.

PRESENTATION OF THE STIMULUS PROGRAMS

Through closed circuit television, we transmitted to our suitably divided audiences either the antisocial WP program ($n = 94$) or the neutral program ($n = 94$). The critical incident of the former appeared in its usual place in the narrative and also at the beginning of the episode, as a teaser. Our intention was to engage the subject's interest from the first moment, and to make sure he saw the critical passage even if he left early, and by repitition to impress it strongly upon him. The most exciting sequence of the neutral program (the one used in Experiment I) was similarly repeated.

RESULTS

The theft rate associated with the antisocial WP-version was 6.4%, somewhat greater than the neutral program's 4.3%, but not significantly so. The other dependent variables yielded similar results. (These unpromising results coupled with our subjects' extremely difficult behavior—urinating on floors, threatening violence to our staff, etc.—together with complaints from other tenants in the building, persuaded us to discontinue this experiment after fewer than 200 trials.)

CONCLUSION

No effect. The opportunity immediately to imitate the antisocial dramatization did not lead to an increase in imitation. But the finding is not without reservation, which arises from the difference between the present test circumstances and the earlier ones. A subject who had seen the stimulus program in a theater had, when he left that setting, no reason to feel that he was still under scrutiny: He had handed in his questionnaire and by that very gesture was done with his role as a member of the test audience. His subsequent visit to the gift center constituted a separate and unconnected event, an impression that intervening time reinforced.

A subject of the present experiment, on the other hand, despite our attempts to create every appearance that he was alone and anonymous, might still feel that he was under scrutiny. In the former case, stimulus and test were well separated; in the present one, they were concurrent. Although some factors in this new situation may have operated to stimulate theft (such as the immediate availability of the charity bank), the heightened fear of scrutiny may have played an inhibitory role.

THE BROADCAST STUDY: NEW YORK

Our data thus far, gleaned from preview theater and closed circuit settings, did not support the imitation hypothesis. But we had
no assurance that we could extrapolate from these atypical viewing
circumstances to home viewing, the focus of our inquiry. And so,
at 9 p.m. on the 21st and 28th of April we broadcast our stimulus
programs over the air. While most of the country saw a neutral episode of *Medical Center*, 1,200,000 viewing homes in the New York
City area saw the version depicting antisocial behavior with punishment.

RECRUITING THE AUDIENCE

To avoid the prohibitive costs of telephone-polling and
telephone-recruiting (which, moreover, carried out at the time of
the program, might have distracted potential subjects from the
critical sequences of our program), we solicited our audiences by
direct mail, though this method, too, detracted somewhat from
the ideal of a wholly natural viewing situation, for it *directed* our
subjects' attention to the program.

On *Television Previews* stationery, we mailed letters to 7000

35

installment-plan buyers, asking them to watch our programs, respond to the few questions enclosed, and bring their answers to the gift center, where they would receive a transistor radio. We did not solicit students, having exhausted that population in our earlier experiments. (See letter, page 37).

We divided our mailing in two: half the letters went to the control group, which, in order to avoid contaminating with the antisocial version, we scheduled first: they would see the neutral program, which was the *Medical Center* episode broadcast a week earlier. The other half of our letters went to the experimental subjects, who were asked to watch the antisocial WP-version, the following week.

SUBJECTS

Our 7000 invitation-questionnaires brought 302 persons to the gift-distribution center, of whom some 60% were male; 23%, black; 30%, under 30; and 10%, over 60. Our final test population, reduced because 63 were in one way or another interrupted at testing time, was 236 (see Table 11).

ASSESSMENT PROCEDURE

We restored our gift-distribution center and submitted both the experimental and control groups to the procedure—and the brusque notice—of our first experiment. And to check that our subjects had indeed seen the stimulus programs, we had them answer a short questionnaire in the exit room, where the radios were distributed.

It is clear from scrutiny of Table 6 that the antisocial program did not stimulate imitation; for while 2.8% of our neutral program subjects broke into the collection box, only .8% of our WP subjects did so.

Interestingly, the total incidence of antisocial behavior in this home-viewing experiment appears to be *less* than that following the preview-theater showings. This result may have arisen purely from chance or from a shift in subject population—those who

Television Previews

Post Office Box 3435, Grand Central Station, New York, New York 10017

Dear Friend,

    You have been selected to take part in a market survey, and as a token of our appreciation for your help, we will award you a new General Electric transistor radio. What we ask you to do is to watch <u>Medical Center</u> on Wednesday, May 12 at 8:00 p.m. on Channel 4, then answer some simple questions about the program. When you return the questionnaire to us you may pick up, without any charge, your General Electric transistor radio.

Here are the questions:

1.   Which character in this episode did you like best?_____

2.   Which scene did you like best?_____

                                  _____

3.   Which commercial appealed to you most?_____

4.   Do you use the product shown in this commercial?_____

5.   How often do you buy this product?_____

6.   Where do you buy it?_____

Your name_____

Address_____

Age____ Sex____ Occupation_____Signature_____

If you watched this program, and only if you watched this program, you may pick up your General Electric transistor radio on Wednesday, May 19,11:00 a.m. 7:00 p.m.

                    AT: Lancelot Products
                        Room 2303 (23rd Floor)
                        130 West 42nd Street
                        New York, New York 10036

Please be certain to bring the questionnaire with you in person. No radios will be distributed to a person who has not seen the program, and a simple recognition test will be given to assure this.

                                    Sincerely,

                                  Gordon Wyeth
                                  Gordon Wyeth

TABLE 6

Proportion of Subjects Performing Antisocial Acts in the
New York Broadcast Study According to Stimulus Program

	Stimulus Program		
	Antisocial WP $n = 127$	Neutral program $n = 109$	Significance of differences[a]
Broke into bank and stole money	.8% (1)	2.8% (3)	n.s.
Removed Dangling Dollar only	2.4% (3)	6.4% (7)	n.s.
Unsuccessfully attempted to break into bank	1.6% (2)	.9% (1)	n.s.
Stole other items from room	3.2% (4)	5.5% (6)	n.s.

$N = 236$

[a]By Fisher Exact Test, $p > .30$ in all cases, n.s.

would respond to a theater invitation versus those who have only to turn on their television sets.

Another factor may have been the theater audience's greater frustration (they had been disappointed both at the theater and by the no-more-radio note, rather than by the note alone), and the cumulative frustration in the preview theater group may have caused their higher incidence of antisocial behavior.

THE BROADCAST STUDY: ST. LOUIS

Having broadcast one antisocial version of our program, in New York, (the version in which Desmond is punished for his crime), we could not use New York City to test our other version, which depicts Desmond's antisocial behavior with *no* punishment (NP). And so we moved to St. Louis, hoping, too, that we might recruit for the experiment larger numbers of subjects than we had in New York. The neutral program was shown in St. Louis on April 12, 1971, and the antisocial version (NP) on April 19.

SUBJECTS

We recruited our audience as we had for Experiment V, the New York televised test; our mailing list, the only one available, was compiled from a telephone directory. In an effort to increase the number of subjects, 12,000 letters, virtually identical to the one used before, were sent out. Five hundred and ninety usable subjects—substantially more than in New York, appeared at the laboratory.

THE GIFT-DISTRIBUTION CENTER

The New York laboratory was packed and shipped to St. Louis. A gift-distribution center/lab was set up on the 9th floor of a downtown office building on Olive Street, a somewhat better neighborhood than West 42nd Street. As in New York, the entire floor was devoted to our study. And the laboratory, consisting of six dummy gift-distribution companies, was operated in the same fashion as in New York.

Scrutiny of Table 7 shows the antisocial program did not produce significantly more antisocial behavior than the neutral program; indeed, not so much as a 1% difference emerged between the two program audiences on any of the dependent variables. Again the overall rate of antisocial action was considerably less than we had obtained in preview theater studies, and perhaps for the same reasons cited in Experiment V.

Our St. Louis test population differed considerably from our New York group. They were less irritable, reacting to the frustrating note more calmly. Moreover, remarks scrawled on the frustrating note in New York were typically unsavory and obscene,

TABLE 7

Proportion of Subjects Performing Antisocial Acts in the St. Louis Broadcast Study According to Stimulus Program[a]

	Stimulus Program		
	Antisocial NP ($n = 282$)	Neutral program ($n = 308$)	Significance of differences $df = 1$
Broke into bank and stole money	1.1% (3)	.7% (2)	n.s.
Removed Dangling Dollar only	1.8% (5)	1.0% (3)	n.s.
Unsuccessfully attempted to break into bank	.4% (1)	1.0% (3)	n.s.
Stole other items from room	2.8% (8)	2.6% (8)	n.s.

$N = 590$.

[a]By Fisher Exact Test, $p > .30$ in all cases.

whereas in St. Louis, comments were characteristically reserved (such as: "I'll call the Better Business Bureau."). The levels of antisocial behavior in St. Louis and New York are about the same; neither shows the influence of the antisocial stimulus program.

THE TELEPHONE STUDY

There is a serious limitation in the experimental model we have worked with thus far. To understand it, we must consider the nature of the mass media. Stimulus content is transmitted to a very large number of people from an emitting source. Several million people across the country watched the *Medical Center* episode used in this study. Influence on only a very small fraction of the viewers could constitute an important *social* fact, but it would not emerge as a statistical fact in the experiment just outlined. For the assessment procedure by its very nature could test only a relatively small sample of those millions.

Let us say, for example, that the antisocial program influenced only one-tenth of 1% of the viewers—one person in a thousand; then fully a thousand of each million who saw it would be affected—a number of obvious social significance. Yet, our methods would not detect this fact because each of our experiments, necessarily limited in the numbers it can deal with, is based upon at most 500 subjects. And although that number is unusually large in terms of social-psychological experimentation, it would not tell the story, for one-tenth of 1% of 500 is *less than a single subject.*

It appears, then, that our method can disclose only much larger effects, those on the order of, say, 10% of the entire viewing audience. On that scale, if a million New Yorkers saw our WP-version, and 100,000 of them imitated the antisocial act, we could with our present methods detect the program's influence. But what if we are dealing with a phenomenon involving only one-hundredth of that number?

To overcome this limitation (1) we could employ extremely large numbers of subjects in the assessment situation, or (2) attempt to locate and use a subject population that was considerably more prone to influence by the media than the general population. A possible third course is to have very good information on *all* the antisocial imitation that occurs after our broadcast, not only in the laboratory but in the community at large. We did, in fact, seek precisely that data from several charity drives that were using collection boxes at the time of our broadcast; but all of them, reluctant to disclose the extent to which their efforts were vitiated by theft, declined to cooperate.

We can summarize the problem by stating that while the stimulus is transmitted to millions, the assessment procedures are geared to several hundred. We need to devise an assessment procedure that is sensitive to the fact that only a small fraction of those exposed to the program may be influenced by it. We need to show on television an antisocial act that anyone viewing in his own home could imitate with impunity, and which, if imitated, would be signaled to us. Toward this end, a second antisocial act was designed into the *Medical Center* episode. Namely, Tom Desmond makes two abusive telephone calls to a medical charity.

Desmond's antisocial use of the phone occurs when he responds to Dr. Gannon's telethon plea for pledges. In the first call, Tom says:

> *Hello, Telethon. I wanna talk to Gannon, Dr. Joseph Gannon ... I got a message for him. Tell him I think his clinic stinks. Tell him it's nothing but a crummy monument to his crummy ego. It . . .*
> (Click at the other end of the line.)

In Tom's second call:

> TOM: *Hello, is Gannon still busy? I wanna talk to him.*
>
> OPERATOR: *He's busy, sir: do you wish to make a contribution?*

TOM: *No, I'm not making any contribution to your stinkin' clinic! How much money you got so far?*

OPERATOR: *I don't have that figure, but if you wish to add to . . .*

TOM: *Well, instead of ADDING money, you can start subtracting. You're gonna start LOSING money any minute now!*
(Tom hangs up.)

The next task, from a technical standpoint, was to provide the viewer with a convenient opportunity to imitate the abusive calls. This was done in the following way: immediately following the *Medical Center* episode, a public service commercial appeared, in which viewers were asked to call in pledges to an authentic medical charity, Project Hope.

The 30-second public service spot, which was sandwiched between commercial messages, featured an attractive Eurasian girl, seated alongside a model of the hospital ship HOPE, and requesting viewers to call in telephone pledges for this charity. Meanwhile, a local telephone number was overlaid on the screen, so that viewers would know what number to call. The girl said:

My name is Kalen
And I want to talk to you about the good ship HOPE.
It's a floating medical center that trains doctors and nurses all over the world.
And it saves lives–thousands of lives.
Project HOPE has special programs in America, too!
But it needs your help.
Call this number and pledge some money.
Call this number and with your pledge.
Bring the world more HOPE.

A bank of telephone operators was trained to receive pledges and to write down all comments made by the callers. The calls were also recorded, a fact that the operators acknowledged by saying:

Thank you for your call, which we will record to insure accuracy. Do you wish to make a pledge to Project Hope?

With the stimulus and appeal broadcast, the opportunity and means for imitation were at hand. If only one-tenth of 1% of the estimated 1,235,000 homes in New York tuned in to *Medical Center* imitated Tom, more than a thousand abusive calls would be forthcoming. We could compare that figure to the response of a control group—a similar audience that saw the public-service message immediately following a neutral *Medical Center* episode the week before. Would the proportion of abusive calls be greater following Tom's example?

(We were aware, of course, that there would be a limitation in our data: the basic unit would be the received telephone call, but we could not know whether a single individual would call a number of times, or whether every call would come from a different person. But since the same possibilities would inhere in the calls following both the stimulus and neutral programs, we would assume that the number of repeat calls is the same in both cases and so cancel each other.)

FIRST TEST

To provide a first test of the procedure, the Project Hope television spot was presented in Chicago and Detroit following *Medical Center* episodes on February 10 (Neutral Episode) and February 17 (Antisocial WP).

We considered the possibility that a person might imitate the antisocial behavior at some point after the commercial was shown. Perhaps there would be a sleeper effect, whereby the influence is not manifested until a period of time elapsed between the showing of the commercial and release of the behavior. To take account of this, two steps were taken.

First, we made certain that some telephone operators would remain on duty for the project for several days after the commercial was shown. Second, in order to stimulate additional calls, advertisements for Project Hope, asking people to call in pledges, were placed in Detroit and Chicago newspapers for several days just prior to each program and for several days after the program (February 7, 9, 12, 14, 16, 19, and 21). However, in order to distinguish between those persons calling in response to the newspaper advertisement, and those calling in response to the television spot,

TABLE 8

Number of Telephone Responses to Project Hope Appeals Following Neutral, Prosocial, and Antisocial WP Programs (Chicago and Detroit)

	Chicago		Detroit	
	Feb. 10 Neutral $n = 19$	Feb. 17 Prosocial $n = 10$	Feb. 10 Neutral $n = 12$	Feb. 17 Antisocial $n = 31$
Clearly antisocial	–	–	–	–
Possibly antisocial	2	–	–	–
Pledge of funds	3	2	3	8
Wants further information	–	–	2	3
Hang up without responding	10	6	3	9
Miscellaneous (wrong number)	1	2	1	3
Child	3	–	3	8
Total:	19	10	12	31

different telephone numbers were used in the newspaper and on the television spot. The experimental program shown in Chicago was the *Prosocial Version,* while the program shown in Detroit was the *Antisocial Version with Punishment.* The prosocial version did not contain any of the telephone sequences. The results are shown in Table 8.

As Table 8 shows, the main problem is that the Project Hope appeals did not create a sufficient number of calls for any meaningful analysis. Of the calls received, only two were ambiguously antisocial, and they followed presentation of the neutral program.

NEW YORK TEST

The test was repeated in New York City, but the procedures were altered in the following way. First, in order to increase the total number of calls that could be analyzed, the Project Hope television spot was repeated several times after the program was shown. Second, in the Chicago and Detroit test, the telephone number appeared on the screen only during the last 10 seconds of the 30-second spot. In New York, we would have the telephone number appear for 25 seconds, and thus give viewers greater opportunity to write down the New York number. Third, in Chicago and Detroit, the telephone calls were recorded, and the callers were informed of this in the operators' introductory remark: "Thank you for your call, which we will record to insure accuracy. Do you wish to make a pledge to Project Hope?" By checking the operators' written accounts in Chicago and Detroit with the recordings, we were satisfied that they had been accurate in recording the telephone comments. We thought that perhaps the announcement of recording the message would inhibit abusive calls. So, in the New York study, we eliminated the announcement and relied exclusively on the written report of the operators.

Finally, to generate more calls, we repeated the Project Hope spot several times after the program had been shown. We broadcast the neutral program on Wednesday, April 14; the antisocial WP-version, the following week, April 21. The Project Hope appeal appeared at the end of *Medical Center* just before 10 p.m.; an hour later, at the end of the following program, *Hawaii Five-O*; again during the 11 o'clock news; and twice more during the *Merv Griffin Show,* a night talk show. We repeated them again on each of the following Fridays, two days after the *Medical Center* presentations: at the end of *The Interns,* during the 11 o'clock news, and twice during *Merv Griffin*—for a grand total of 18 times, enough, we hoped, to generate a sufficient number of calls for statistical analysis.

There remains the question, of course, of how many persons who saw the original *Medical Center* episode were also likely to see the spots. According to the A. C. Nielsen Company, 23.7% of the 5,200,000 television homes in the New York area were tuned in to *Medical Center* (at least during its last quarter-hour) on April 21, when the antisocial WP-version and the first set of Project Hope appeals appeared. And between 70 and 90% of those who saw the subsequent spots had also seen the program; e.g., 85% of those who saw the spot during the 11 o'clock news had also seen the critical *Medical Center* segment.[1]

---

[1]Data based on the Nielsen Station Index New York Instantaneous Audimeter, April 21, 1971. Data subject to qualifications.

TABLE 9

Telephone Responses to Project Hope Appeals following Neutral and Antisocial WP Programs in New York

	Stimulus Program		Significance of $df = 1$
	Neutral ($n = 124$)	Antisocial WP ($n = 69$)	
Clearly antisocial	6 (4.8%)	4 (5.8%)	$\chi^2 = .00$ n.s.
Possibly antisocial	14 (11.3%)	4 (5.8%)	$\chi^2 = 1.00$ n.s.
Pledge of funds	15 (12.1%)	14 (20.3%)	$\chi^2 = 1.73$ n.s.
Wants further information	14 (11.3%)	10 (14.5%)	$\chi^2 = .18$ n.s.
Hang up without response	60 (48.4%)	34 (49.3%)	$\chi^2 = .00$ n.s.
Miscellaneous (includes children, but not antisocial)	15 (12.1%)	3 (4.4%)	$\chi^2 = 2.30\ p < .13$
Total:	124	69	

RESULTS

A total of 193 telephone calls were received in response to the Project Hope spots in New York, 124 in the week in which the neutral version of the program was presented, and 69 in the week in which the antisocial version was presented. The data are shown in Table 9.

More calls came in during the first week, when the neutral program was shown. What seems likely is that many of the same persons watch the program from one week to the next, and those primed to call in to a Project Hope commercial, do so when the first appeal is presented. Thus, the control program siphoned off some of those who, had there been no control, would have called in response to the second program.

The clearly antisocial calls for the neutral program were:

1. I'll make a pledge if you tell me how many hairs you have on your cunt.
2. I'll make a pledge in your vagina.
3. Pussy!
4. Would you like to see my dick?
5. You're ugly.
6. You can't spell, what are you, stupid? (said to operator when asked for name).

The clearly antisocial calls for the antisocial program were:

1. That chink is ugly.
2. Up yours.
3. Lousy commercial.
4. What size tits?

We did not find an increase in percentage of abusive calls resulting from the program. Indeed, as we analyze the language of those calls that did come in, we see that not one of them actually imitates Tom Desmond's language. There is no use of the words "stinkin' crummy ego," nor does any caller threaten to diminish the money of Project Hope. Rather, we find a small array of sexually abusive comments that in no way seems to have been increased by the program.[2]

It is possible, of course, that a more interesting or stimulating antisocial action by Desmond would have inspired more imitation. If, for example—and this is purely speculative—we had shown him dialing a number that released the money in a pay phone, thousands of viewers might have dialed that number. It is also possible that the call he did make did not integrate into the motives of potentially antisocial viewers. The motives for breaking into a charity box seem clear enough if one is poor and needs money; the motives for making an abusive call are less so.

Of course, telephone calls reported in the mass media sometimes do appear to inspire imitation. The announcement on a television newscast of a few bomb threats seems to be dismayingly fruitful: as many as 4000 calls have clogged the New York City Police Department's switchboard on such occasions.

The differences between such perversely inspiring stimuli and those of our experiment are not entirely clear, though two points are worth noting. First, newscasts of bomb threats refer to real events, not to theatrical fictions, and may for that reason be more potent; and second, the gratification for calling in a bomb threat may not reside in the verbal delivery of the message, but in viewing

[2]The identical analysis was performed on the calls that came in response to the Project Hope spot immediately following the neutral and experimental programs. Since these were closest in time to the program, we thought they might be more likely to show imitation. But this was not the case. Twenty-four calls came in immediately after the neutral episode, with one clearly antisocial, and two possibly antisocial messages. Thirty-six calls immediately followed the antisocial *Medical Center* broadcast, with one antisocial message.

its consequences, that is, the arrival of the police, clearing of the building, etc.

It is possible, also, that the abusive calls stimulated by the program were deflected to some other organization, and that somewhere in the city, a charity drive was receiving many antisocial comments stimulated by the program. But this is speculation, and in any case, we ought to have received at least a portion of those calls. We certainly made it easy enough for the stimulated subject to direct his abusive comments at Project Hope.

So far as the method used here is concerned, we believe that it is a promising one. It is potentially a very sensitive procedure and, possibly with some change in the stimulus material, could demonstrate imitative effects. In any case, it is clear from the experiment that not just any antisocial action shown on a single television program is likely to produce imitation. If this were so, we would have received hundreds of abusive calls in imitation of Tom Desmond's action on television. More than a million people saw the program in the New York City area, but our data show that the program had no effect in stimulating imitation of his action.

THE EVENING NEWS STUDY

The subjects of our foregoing experiments had seen our models of antisocial behavior in theaters, at home, and on simulated, closed circuit broadcasts. But however varied the viewing circumstances, the programs themselves were presented as dramatized fiction. Perhaps real-life events are more likely to be imitated than dramatized ones. We set out now to test this possibility, by presenting the antisocial act *as if* it were an actual rather than a fictional event. Our site was, again, New York City; our medium, a closed circuit television newscast.

RECRUITING THE AUDIENCE

Using *Television Research Associates* stationery, we sent 7500 direct-mail invitations to a list of recent high school graduates (the lists exhausted in our previous experiments having been by this time reconstituted), promising a transistor radio if they would appear at the Statler-Hilton hotel and tell us what they thought of a news program and some commercials they would see. We netted 619 subjects. All our subjects were high school seniors: male 556 (89.8%), female 63 (10.2%); black 158 (25.5%), white 453 (73.2%), other 8 (1.3%).

After arriving at the Statler-Hilton office of *Television Research Associates,* subjects were individually assigned to one or another of 16 guest rooms. The room was entirely conventional, with a convertible couch, tables, television set, and wall paintings. In one corner of the room, resting on a table, was a small charity display for the March of Dimes, including a clear plastic collection box containing 40 pennies, a $5 bill, and a protruding single—the Dangling Dollar. (We eliminated the latter after 25 sessions—half the total number—because conversations among the subjects indicated that some thought our procedure was a test of their honesty.)

A message flickering on each room's television screen stated:

PLEASE BE SEATED. PROGRAM TO APPEAR SOON.

(This message, like the news program he would see, was carried to the set by closed circuit cables.)

Soon, an announcer's voice was heard over the television set:

> This is Robert Lance speaking for Television Research Associates. Thank you for coming and offering to give us your opinion of a television news program and some of the commercials that go along with the program.
>
> As you know, the people connected with TV are very interested in audience reaction to their programs. Often, they will bring large audiences together in an auditorium to find out audience opinion. Today, Television Research Associates is trying to check out your opinion in a setting that is more natural than an auditorium, more natural for viewing television.
>
> In a few minutes you will see a fifteen-minute segment of the evening news. We are interested in your reaction to the program, and to the commercials, too. So sit back and enjoy the program. One further point. You were told you would be awarded a radio for coming here. Some of you may wonder if you will receive the radio today. The answer is "no." We do not have the radios here for you. If you follow the instructions care-

fully, the radio will be sent to you sometime within the next two months.

The program will appear shortly.

The message was designed to communicate information about the ostensible purpose of the experiment, and introduce an element of frustration, which we had found necessary to obtain a measurable incidence of theft.

THE NEWS PROGRAM

The following news story, filmed for the purposes of the experiment, was inserted into a videotape of a local news program, and transmitted to our subjects on closed circuit television:

> A reporter, microphone in hand, appears beside a badly smashed Project Hope display. The reporter states that displays of this sort have been placed around the city, and have been smashed and rifled in alarming degree.
>
> The reporter then interviews a Project Hope official, who states that thefts of the banks are so widespread that receipts have declined in relation to those of last year.
>
> To investigate the problem first hand, the reporter states, the "action news team" placed one of the displays on a busy midtown street, and filmed what happened with a hidden camera. There follows a film clip in which, out of a throng of passersby, one man approaches the charity display, removes a tool from his pocket, and begins to pry it open. In a few seconds, he removes the dollar bill, and vanishes into the crowd.
>
> "They say that charity begins at home," the reporter sums up, "but not, apparently, if our home is New York City." A commercial follows, and the news program continues with other items of local news.

Thus, the subject is now presented with a model of antisocial behavior which is treated as having actually occurred,

TABLE 10

Proportion of Subjects Performing Antisocial Acts in the Evening News Study According to Stimulus Program

	Antisocial program			Neutral program		
	Stole all money	Stole Dang-ling Dollar	n	Stole all money	Stole Dang-ling Dollar	n
Tested with Dangling Dollar	6.5% (10)	9.7% (15)	154	12.1% (19)	4.5% (7)	157
Tested without Dangling Dollar	8.6% (13)	not applicable	152	12.2% (19)	not applicable	156
All subjects	7.5% (23)	not applicable	306	12.1% (38)	not applicable	313

$N = 619$

rather than a dramatized fiction. Moreover, he learns from the news story that the antisocial behavior in question is widespread.

The subjects were divided into experimental and control groups, 306 subjects seeing the critical news episode, and 313 subjects seeing the news program without the critical episode.

The data presented in Table 10 reveal conflicting trends. They show, on the one hand, that those who saw the neutral program committed more thefts of all money than those who saw the televised thievery ($\chi^2 = 3.22$, $df = 1$, $p < .08$). On the other hand, they also suggest that more of those who saw the antisocial version stole Dangling Dollars than those who saw the neutral program ($\chi^2 = 2.54$, $df = 1$, $p < .12$). We thus have conflicting evidence on the effect of the newscast.

Of course, the Dangling Dollar and "stole all money" categories are not logically independent. A person who has stolen all the money has also taken the Dangling Dollar, although we have not counted him as doing so. Thus, the apparent higher influence of Dangling Dollar thefts in the experimental program may be a purely residual effect. There is a certain pool of potential thieves: if they are used up through taking all the money, they are no longer available to steal the Dangling Dollar.

How can we explain the lessened breakage in the neutral program? Are we dealing with catharsis? We doubt it, but think the explanation represents a possible artifact. The very fact that a person believes he is being tested for honesty is likely to inhibit antisocial behavior. And the presence of a news story showing theft from a charity box, combined with the actual presence of a charity box in the hotel room, was likely to engender a higher degree of suspicion in the experimental than the control subjects. This may have accounted for the lesser amount of breakage in the experimental group.

Indeed, informal interviews with subjects in the last 25 sessions reveals that about twice as many subjects in the experimental group thought the study had something to do with honesty—compared to those not exposed to the television depicted theft.

There is, furthermore, a feature of the stimulus material that may also have reduced its effectiveness as a model. We thought it would be well to show an actual incident of a person breaking into a charity display, an action model, which we achieved through the hidden camera story. However, the effect of mentioning the "hidden camera" may have been to arouse anxiety in subjects that their own behavior was surreptitiously under scrutiny. After all, the television depicted theft was "exposed," and fear of exposure may function in a powerfully inhibitory manner. It should be noted that this effect need not be limited to behavior in an experiment; knowledge of the fact that some banks have continuous photographic records of customer transactions, may serve to inhibit potential bank robbers, quite outside an experimental context.

The Evening News Study yielded contradictory findings, and the results are, at best, equivocal.

DEMOGRAPHIC ANALYSIS

We have found very little evidence, thus far, that witnessing an antisocial act on television engenders its imitation among viewers. But we have been examining the effects of our stimulus programs on the subject population as a whole. It is possible that imitative effects were produced in some segments of the population, but not in others.

We shall examine the data in terms of standard sociological categories of age, sex, race, education, and occupation. This information is presented for all experiments in Table 11.

Information on these variables was obtained at two points in the study. First, when the subject filled out the questionnaire at the preview theater; and second, based on description of the subject when he came to the gift-distribution center, and was observed on closed circuit television.

One technical problem is that when we partition subjects into demographic groups (young, old, etc.), the numbers within each group are too small for reliable statistical analysis. One way to handle this is to collapse the data over identical experimental conditions, and perform analyses on the pooled data. Three of our experiments had identical component conditions. These are Experiment I, the high frustration condition in

Experiment II, and the no-modeling condition in Experiment III. Pooling all of the subjects in these conditions gives us a total pool of 619 subjects, which can be partitioned for demographic analysis.[1]

RACE

Of the subjects in the pooled population, 28.6% were black, and they contributed to 28.3% of the theft rates (of all money). But our major question is whether the stimulus programs influenced the black subjects. Let us therefore examine the theft rates in conditions I, II, and III for black subjects only.

Table 12 shows that in each of the three conditions more black subjects who were exposed to the antisocial WP-version of the program broke into the donation boxes than those who had seen only the neutral program. The numbers are very small, of course, but in the aggregate 9.0% of the blacks who saw the antisocial program did so, compared to 1.6% for the neutral program. This trend does not attain the conventionally accepted level of significance ($p = .12$, Fisher exact test).

Moreover, the results for the Dangling Dollar go in the opposite direction, leaving the overall picture very unclear (11.5% Dangling Dollar theft rate in the neutral program versus 1.5% in the antisocial WP-version ($p = .06$, Fisher). (The reader is referred to discussion of the Dangling Dollar variable on p. 54.)

The data comparing blacks in the antisocial NP-version versus neutral conditions show the same trends, at a nonsignificant level. When we look at the black response to the program as actually televised in New York and St. Louis, the evidence is totally equivocal, owing to the small number of black subjects in these conditions.

---

[1]When we examine the antisocial NP condition, our pooled data consists only of the subjects in Experiments I and II, since there was no NP condition in Experiment III. At times, this forces us to present two separate tables, one for the WP condition and one for the NP condition. For economy, we only present the NP table when it contributes to the interpretation of the results.

TABLE 11

Population Profiles[a]

Experiment[b]	I	II	III	IV	V	VI
Total (N)	289	488	238	188	236	590
Male	261 [90.31]	402 [82.23]	193 [81.09]	168 [89.36]	144 [61.02]	302 [51.19]
Female	28 [9.69]	86 [17.17]	45 [18.91]	20 [10.64]	92 [38.98]	288 [48.81]
Race						
Black	65 [22.49]	139 [28.48]	98 [41.18]	48 [25.53]	55 [23.31]	85 [14.41]
White	216 [74.74]	344 [70.49]	134 [56.30]	133 [70.74]	178 [75.42]	503 [82.25]
Other	8 [2.77]	5 [1.03]	6 [2.52]	7 [3.72]	3 [1.27]	2 [.34]
Age						
10–19	44 [15.22]	172 [35.25]	8 [3.36]	32 [17.02]	15 [6.35]	17 [2.88]
20–29	90 [31.14]	67 [13.73]	52 [21.85]	82 [43.62]	56 [23.73]	82 [13.90]
30–39	65 [22.49]	72 [14.75]	54 [22.69]	20 [10.64]	53 [22.46]	78 [13.22]
40–49	41 [14.19]	64 [13.11]	43 [18.07]	17 [9.04]	54 [22.88]	120 [20.34]
50–59	39 [13.49]	60 [12.30]	41 [17.23]	8 [4.26]	33 [13.98]	154 [26.10]
60–69	6 [2.08]	41 [8.40]	29 [12.18]	8 [4.26]	17 [7.20]	104 [17.63]
70–79	1 [.35]	12 [2.46]	8 [3.36]	3 [1.60]	7 [2.97]	33 [5.60]
80–89	—	—	1 [.42]	—	1 [.42]	2 [.34]
No answer	3 [1.04]	—	2 [.84]	18 [9.57]	—	—

Education[c]

Elementary	9	[3.11]	15	[3.07]	23	[9.66]	7	[3.72]
JHS	28	[9.69]	40	[8.20]	11	[4.62]	10	[5.32]
HS	104	[35.99]	252	[51.64]	100	[42.02]	53	[28.19]
2 yrs coll	46	[15.92]	47	[9.63]	37	[15.55]	47	[25.00]
4 yrs coll	48	[16.61]	35	[7.17]	29	[12.18]	23	[12.23]
Grad/Profl	42	[14.53]	25	[5.12]	32	[13.45]	12	[6.38]
No answer	12	[4.15]	74	[15.16]	6	[2.52]	36	[19.15]

Occupation[c]

Student	40	[13.84]	150	[30.67]	14	[5.88]	42	[22.34]
Unemployed	6	[2.08]	6	[1.23]	2	[.84]	7	[3.72]
White coll	91	[31.49]	76	[15.54]	61	[25.63]	35	[18.62]
Blue coll	67	[23.18]	108	[22.09]	109	[45.80]	40	[21.28]
Profl	56	[19.38]	22	[4.50]	15	[6.30]	7	[3.72]
Housewife	10	[3.46]	21	[4.29]	14	[5.88]	1	[.53]
Retired	—	[—]	22	[4.50]	12	[5.04]	6	[3.19]
No answer	19	[6.57]	84	[17.17]	11	[4.62]	50	[26.60]

[a]Figures include only those subjects who did not during the experiments encounter other subjects. The numbers in brackets are percentages.

[b]No demographic data available on Experiment VII, The Telephone Study. All subjects of Experiment VIII, The Evening News Study, were high school seniors: see page 52 for sex and race data.

[c]Data not included.

TABLE 12

Theft of Money by Black Subjects as a Function of Stimulus Program

	Stimulus Program					
	Neutral			Antisocial (WP)		
Experimental condition	Stole all money		Stole Dangling dollar *n*	Stole all money		Stole Dangling dollar *n*
Experiment I	0	(0)	6.7% (1) 15	11.1% (2)		0 (0) 18
Experiment II	4.2%	(1)	16.7% (4) 24	8.3% (2)		0 (0) 24
Experiment III	0	(0)	9.1% (2) 22	8.0% (2)		4.0% (1) 25
Total	1.6%	(1)	11.5% (7) 61	9.0% (6)		1.5% (1) 67

SEX

Women accounted for 15.4% of the pooled subject population; they committed 10.6% of the thefts of all money; no discernible influence by the stimulus program, as Table 13 shows.

OCCUPATION

Subjects in the pooled group were classified into the following occupational types: student, blue collar worker, white collar worker, professional, housewife, unemployed, and retired.

Among white collar workers, the antisocial WP-version yielded somewhat more thefts from the charity display than the neutral version (10.2% versus 1.7%, $p = .11$, Fisher). The two

TABLE 13

Breaking into Charity Bank by Sex as a Function of Stimulus Program

	Stimulus Program			
Sex	Neutral	*n*	Antisocial (WP)	*n*
Male	5.6% (10)	179	5.6% (11)	195
Female	4.8% (2)	42	3.1% (1)	32

TABLE 14

Breaking into Charity Bank among White Collar Workers as a Function of Stimulus Program

Experimental condition	Stimulus Program				
	Neutral		n	Antisocial WP	n
Experiment I	0	(0)	23	11.1% (3)	27
Experiment II	4.4%	(1)	23	7.2% (1)	14
Experiment III	0	(0)	12	11.1% (2)	18
Total	1.7%	(1)	58	10.2% (6)	59

programs had an opposite effect on students; 16.7% of the students viewing the neutral version broke into the display, whereas only 2.6% of those viewing the WP-version did so ($p = .11$, Fisher), as Tables 14 and 15 show. Perhaps students in the antisocial WP condition were suspicious, while students in the neutral condition were not, and suspicion may have led to a suppression of theft.

The unpunished antisocial version did not produce a significant effect either in the case of students or white collar workers. For white collar workers, neutral versus antisocial NP: 2.9% versus 2.2%; for students, 9.3% versus 17.7%.

On the televised program, there was insufficient breakage to discern any trend. There were no discernible effects of the stimulus program for any other occupational groups.

TABLE 15

Breaking into Charity Bank among Students as a Function of Stimulus Program

Experimental condition	Stimulus Program				
	Neutral		n	Antisocial WP	n
Experiment I	10.8%	(1)	10	0 (0)	8
Experiment II	20.8%	(5)	24	3.7% (1)	27
Experiment III	0	(0)	2	0 (0)	4
Total	16.7%	(6)	36	2.6% (1)	39

TABLE 16

Breaking into Charity Bank by Age and According to Stimulus Program

	\(Age\) 16–19	n	20–29	n	30–39	n	40–49	n	50–59	n	60–80	n
Neutral	15.4% (6)	39	0 (0)	49	0 (0)	40	9.1% (3)	33	5.9% (2)	34	3.8% (1)	(26)
Antisocial	7.0% (3)	43	2.4% (1)	42	3.5% (3)	58	2.9% (1)	35	10.7% (3)	28	4.8% (1)	(21)

AGE AND EDUCATION

Subjects were classified by age, as shown in Table 16. Teen-agers constituted 22% of the pooled subject population, but they committed 40% of the breakage of the bank, a propor-tion almost twice as great as their numbers would suggest ($\chi^2 = 5.94$, $df = 1$, $p < .02$). This accords with national crime statistics (Uniform Crime Reports, 1970). But none of the age groups is significantly affected by the stimulus programs. Thus, among teenagers, 15.4% exposed to the neutral program broke into the bank, while 7.0% who had seen the antisocial WP con-dition did so (n.s., Fisher). Similar results were obtained for teenagers watching the NP-version, though again at a non-significant level (17.5% versus 9.6%).

Subjects were also classified in terms of the highest level of schooling they had attained, but again, we found no effect of the stimulus program.

PERSONS WHO IDENTIFIED WITH TOM

At the preview theater subjects were asked questions about the program they had seen. Among the questions was: "Which of the characters shown in the television program is most like you?" We thought that viewers who identified with Tom Desmond might be more prone to commit antisocial acts than those identifying with other characters. However, we did not find this to be the case. Of those identifying with Tom (a total of 11.3% of the subjects), 4.6% broke into the charity bank, while 4.4% of those identifying with other characters did so, in the antisocial WP audiences. Similar nonsignificant effects were noted in the NP condition.

TIME DELAY

Subjects had entered the assessment situation 1 to 7 days after being exposed to the stimulus films. We had attempted,

TABLE 17

Breaking into Charity Bank as a Function of the Number of Days Intervening between Exposure to Stimulus Program and Assessment Situation[a]

	Number of days						
	1	2	3	4	5	6	7
Neutral	2.0% (1/49)	13.2% (5/38)	0% (0/17)	6.9% (2/29)	0% (0/14)	8.3% (3/36)	4.6% (1/22)
Antisocial	0% (0/48)	14.3% (4/28)	3.2% (1/31)	14.8% (4/27)	0% (0/17)	3.5% (1/29)	5.7% (2/35)
Total	1.0% (1/97)	13.6% (9/66)	2.1% (1/48)	10.7% (6/56)	0% (0/31)	6.2% (4/65)	5.3% (3/57)

[a]Comparisons between neutral and antisocial program were tested for each day by Fisher exact test and prove to be nonsignificant.

in Experiments III and IV to deal with the effects of delay. But we can also analyze the proportion of antisocial acts committed as a function of the days intervening between the exposure to the stimulus film and appearance at the gift-distribution center.

Representative data are shown in Table 17. Analysis shows that the passage of time does not interact with the stimulus materials in a way that affects the level of antisocial behavior.

In sum, the analysis of results of black subjects, white collar workers, and students showing possible influence of the stimulus program are suggestive and ought to constitute a starting point for further inquiry. These trends emerged only late in our study when it was not possible to run further experiments. Obviously, the next step is to repeat the study using large numbers of subjects drawn from these groups.

But, in truth, we lack confidence in the stability of the findings as they now stand. The data constitute the basis of a hypothesis, rather than reliable conclusions.

CONCLUSIONS

This research started with the idea that viewers imitate some of the antisocial action they see on television. We set out to measure actual imitation of a television depicted act. We created a program in which the act—breaking into a charity bank—is shown repeatedly, and with considerable dramatic impact. We created an assessment situation in which antisocial acts and imitation could easily occur.

In a first experiment, subjects saw one of four stimulus programs in a preview theater, and were then tested at a gift-distribution center. Result: a trend, though not statistically significant, that one of the anti-social programs engendered imitation. We wondered whether the high level of frustration experienced by the subjects obscured the effects of the stimulus program; we eliminated frustration in Experiment II. Result: no evidence of imitation. We thought a model, or booster placed in the assessment situation, might interact with the stimulus program and produce an effect. Result: negative. We reduced the time delay between seeing the television act and the occasion for imitating it, by embedding both in the same situation. Result: negative. We broadcast the stimulus material in New York and St. Louis and again sought to measure imita-

tion, but there was none. We changed the material from dramatized fiction to real life incidents presented on the news. Result:
no imitation. We adopted a new paradigm of investigation
in the telephone study, by giving an opportunity to any viewer
to immediately imitate the act by calling in an abusive message.
We hoped this would be a very sensitive measure that could
pick up even slight effects. But again, we found no evidence
that the antisocial program engendered imitation. We looked
for effects in subpopulations, and here the results were equivocal.
We did our best to find imitative effects, but all told, our search
yielded negative results.

Two quite different interpretations of the results are possible: First, the programs did, in reality, stimulate a tendency
in our subjects to perform antisocial acts, but our measurement
procedures were deficient. Second, there was no imitative tendency induced by the program.

Let us consider the first possibility: The program had a potential
for inducing imitation. Why might we have missed it?

First, the imitative response may occur in the subject at
another point in time or space, and not within the assessment
situation we had set up. Perhaps, a year from now, a subject on
the threshold of breaking into a charity bank, will be influenced
by the program.

Second, perhaps we did not test the right subject population.
Conceivably, people below the minimum age for this study would
have been measurably influenced by the program. We chose to
limit our subject population out of practical considerations
and because we did not want to provoke mere children into
imitating antisocial behavior. (Of course, we did study teenagers, but, conceivably, television affects even younger children.)

Or, perhaps in the very process of recruiting subjects for our
study, we eliminated those most likely to have been influenced
by the program. It requires a certain discipline to come to a
preview theater, fill out a gift certificate, and then show up
at the gift-distribution center. Perhaps some delinquents in
the population were excluded by this procedure. However, the
fact that we did get considerable antisocial behavior in the laboratory does, somewhat, weaken this argument.

Fourth, it is possible that the program stimulates imitation
in only a very small fraction of the viewing audience, and we

could not pick this up with the numbers used in our assessment procedures. However, we did introduce the telephone procedure to get around this, though using a quite different antisocial act. Perhaps if we could combine the sensitivity of the telephone measure with the motivational properties of the theft measure, an effect might have been discovered.

And, of course, we can go on endlessly. For when an experiment yields no differences between the experimental and control conditions, there is an infinitude of factors that may account for this. However, these are merely speculations, and do not have the status of evidence until they are themselves converted to tested operations. Often we ourselves thought we had figured out why we were not getting imitative effects, converted this notion into an experiment, only to fail again in our search for an effect.

Let us assume now that our measuring procedure is completely adequate and that, in fact, the stimulus material does not induce imitation. This would still not mean, however, that television does not stimulate antisocial behavior. Let us consider the factors not treated by the experiments described here.

1. It is possible that the television depiction of a different antisocial action would have engendered imitation. Perhaps, an antisocial act that contains the germ of a new criminal technique is more likely to be imitated. Note the series of parachute hijacks that appears to have been, in part, due to the dissemination of this technique by the mass media.

2. Perhaps it is not so much the depiction of one antisocial act, as the cumulative impact of numerous violent actions shown on television, from childhood onward, that predisposes a person to commit antisocial behavior. Conceivably, our subjects have been so sated with the depiction of crime on television, that they are already maximally stimulated, and our program can add no further to it.

3. Or a more indirect mechanism may be at work, namely, that the norms and attitudes of society are changed by the frequent depiction of violence, so that even a person who has not viewed television, will be influenced by it through his absorption of general societal attitudes.

4. Perhaps the manner in which Desmond breaks into the charity banks did not stimulate imitation, because his actions were depicted dramatically rather than casually.

All of these possibilities exist, but are outside the scope of the present investigation. We can only urge that other investigators apply themselves to the study of these variables.

What then is the contribution of the present study. First, the evidence it has generated must be taken seriously, and serve as a constraint on discussion of television's effects. For the results of the present experiment are not that we obtained *no findings,* but rather that we obtained *no differences* in those exposed to our different stimulus programs. The research thus consistently supports the null hypothesis (see p. 59f for possible exceptions).

It is possible that people have been entirely too glib in discussing the negative social consequences of the depiction of television violence. Personally, the investigators find the constant depiction of violence on television repugnant. But that is quite different from saying it leads to antisocial behavior among its viewers. We have not been able to find evidence for this; for if television is on trial, the judgment of this investigation must be the Scottish verdict: Not proven.

Second, we hope the study has cleared the way methodologically for much new research. We believe that the general experimental paradigms presented here are by no means exhausted in the present investigation. The use of new stimulus material, younger populations, and modified assessment procedures can only further our knowledge of television's effects. The telephone study, though yielding no evidence of imitation in the present investigation, does point to the kind of experimental paradigm needed for further inquiry.

Not that the present paradigm is the only useful approach. Far from it. We carried it out because it seemed to us logical to start with a single program; if we could have demonstrated imitative effects in this single program, we could without equivocation have concluded that television stimulates antisocial behavior. That we did not find an effect does not exclude this possibility. We believe that future inquiry should direct itself to the long range effects of television, of many programs, over time.

Finally, in this research, a major television network extended its resources to social scientists wishing to study the possible effects of television depicted antisocial behavior. We regard this, not as the fulfillment of television obligations to society, but as a firm precedent, on which future investigation shall move ahead.

REFERENCES

Asch, S. E. Studies of independence and conformity: A minority of one against a unanimous majority. *Psychological Monographs, 70* (9), 1956.

Baker, R. K. & Ball, S. J. *Violence and the Media.* Washington, D.C., National Commission on the Causes and Prevention of Violence, 1969.

Bandura, A. What TV violence can do to your child. *Look,* October 22, 1963, 46–52.

Bandura, A., Ross, D., & Ross, S. Imitation of film-mediated aggressive models. *Journal of Abnormal and Social Psychology,* 1963, **67**, 601–607.

Barcus, F. E. 1971. Cited in United States Public Health Service. Report to the Surgeon General. *Television and growing up: The impact of televised violence.* (Superintendent of Documents, U.S. Government Printing Office, 1972)

Berkowitz, L. Violence in the mass media. In Berkowitz, L. (Ed.), *Aggression.* New York: McGraw-Hill, 1962.

Dollard, J., Doob, I. W., Miller, N. E., Mowrer, O. H., & Sears, R. R. *Frustration and aggression.* New Haven: Yale Univ. Press, 1939.

Feshbach, S. & Singer, R. D. *Television and aggression.* San Francisco: Josey-Bass, 1971.

Gerbner, G. 1971. Cited in United States Public Health Service Report to the Surgeon General. *Television and growing up: The Impact of televised violence.* (Superintendent of Documents, U.S. Government Printing Office, 1972.)

Hartley, R. E. A review and evaluation of recent studies on the impact of violence. Office of Social Research, C.B.S., June 24, 1964. Mimeo.

Himmelweit, H., Oppenheim, A. N., & Vance, P. *Television and the child: An empirical study of television viewing on the young.* New York: Oxford Univ. Press, 1958.

Latané, B. & Darley, J. M. *The unresponsive bystander: Why doesn't he help?* New York: Appleton, 1970.

Milgram, S. Some conditions of obedience and disobedience to authority. *Human Relations,* 1965, **18** (1), 57–76.

Singer, J. L. (Ed.) *The control of aggression and violence: Cognitive and physiological factors.* New York: Academic Press, 1971.

Uniform Crime Reports 1970. *Federal Bureau of Investigation, United States Department of Justice,* Washington, D.C. (Superintendent of Documents, U.S. Government Printing Office.)

United States Public Health Service. *Television and social behavior: An annotated bibliography of research focusing on television's impact on children.* National Institute of Mental Health, 1971.

United States Public Health Service. Report to the Surgeon General. *Television and growing up: The impact of television violence.* (Superintendent of Documents, U. S., Government Printing Office, 1972.)

APPENDIX I

BRIEF HISTORY OF THE RESEARCH

S. Milgram

This project originated in a meeting of social scientists called by the Office of Social Research of The Columbia Broadcasting System, attended by the senior author. My first conception of how a study ought to be carried out called for the creation of communities that are free of any violence shown on television, and the study of crime statistics in these communities over a period of years. But the technical problems of carrying out a study of this sort are almost insurmountable, and the plan was shelved.

A more manageable approach could be achieved by retaining the principle of experimental logic, but limiting it to the use of a single stimulus program. The idea would be to show some antisocial act on television, then test its effects in the community. A research proposal along this line was formally submitted to the Office of Social Research at CBS, and, after submission to a review board of social scientists, approved.

The next year was spent finding a suitable program that could serve the purpose of the experiment. Several routes were taken, to make certain that at least one of them would succeed. Finally, a meeting was arranged with the producers of *Medical Center*. The two producers of the that program, Frank Glicksman and Al Ward, agreed to cooperate in the production of the needed stimulus program, with its several variant endings.

73

The meeting took place in December 1969, and the next months were spent in correspondence with Don Brinkley, who wrote the script according to the experimental specifications, in three versions. Finally, the program was ready to go into production, and I sat on the sidelines at MGM studios acting as a censor whenever an element was introduced that did not meet the needs of the experiment. The effort was relatively successful, but there were two major problems in the production of the stimulus programs:

1. The programs were produced in the normal Hollywood fashion, which entailed a lack of flexibility. Once filmed, programs could not be refilmed except at enormous expense. In an ordinary experiment, an investigator may try one particular stimulus, and if he does not like it, or does not get the effects he thinks he should get, he may change or modify it. This luxury was not available in this investigation. Once the programs were set, we had to carry out our investigation using them as our basic tools.

2. The second problem was that the investigator's control over the creation of the stimulus programs was not total. The program had to conform to commercial entertainment standards. Furthermore, making a film is a collaborative undertaking involving a scriptwriter, director, and numerous technicians. At points in the production of the film, I found myself up against long-established traditions of directing and acting that, because of the group norms of the production team, became virtually impossible to change.

The points in the film where the experimenter's wishes did not prevail are these: first, in the antisocial version without punishment the experimenter wanted Tom to carry out the antisocial acts with total impunity. However, the director insisted on inserting a chase scene, in which Tom escapes, simply for the purpose of livening up the action. Long discussions with the director could not persuade him to eliminate the chase, and for this reason the antisocial version without punishment is of marginal value. Second, when Tom makes his abusive telephone call in the bar, there is faint trace of inebriation which the experimenter wished eliminated, but which remains in the final print. Third, when Tom breaks into the charity boxes in the bar and tobacco shop, other characters become aware of what he is doing—it would have been preferable if he had done these things totally unobserved.

Despite these deficiencies, the act of breaking into the charity box is presented with great drama and impact. Moreover, it is repeated five times within the course of the film, thus contributing to its memorability. So, on the whole the stimulus materials constituted a forceful, if imperfect, translation into dramatic terms of the experimental ideas.

The next stage of the research concerned the actual assessment of the programs' effects, and it was necessary to create an efficient staff. I recruited Dr. Lance Shotland, then of Michigan State University, as my research associate. Dr. Shotland was to become intimately involved in the project's scientific decisions; he played an especially important part in the decision to carry our Experiments II and III, contributed to the format of all experiments, and throughout carried a good deal of the burden of assessment procedure.

We were aided by Mr. Herman Staudenmayer, now of the University of Colorado, who frequently supervised the field laboratories, and whose skills greatly contributed to the successful execution of the project.

It can truly be said that this project was a team effort. By the time the project was ready for the St. Louis study, it consisted of a skilled research group that could move into the city and within a short time set up complicated laboratory procedures, assess the behavior of several hundred subjects, dismantle, and return to New York.

Not that the study was without problems. At one point the crises were coming to my desk thick and fast. Supplies that were vitally needed for the study had not yet arrived; a national magazine was on the verge of doing a story on the project just days before it was to be carried out on national television; internal problems with some of the cooperating organizations were about to call halt to the entire research enterprise; and all the while, commitments had to be made months in advance to theaters, newspapers, and realtors, and the entire effort brought together in a workable, logistical plan.

The experiments were carried out from September, 1970, through November, 1971; the statistical analysis of results were supervised by Dr. Shotland with the assistance of Herman Staudenmayer and John Sabini. The preparation of the written report was greatly aided by Mr. Lawrence Sandek, a science writer, who prepared an important intermediate version of the report, that greatly improved the exposition.

There is a major section of the original research proposal that was not carried out, and there was a major part of the research not originally mentioned in the proposal. One part of the research proposal called for the placement of charity displays around the city, and to study whether destruction rates changed after the stimulus program was shown on commercial television. Attorneys indicated that this procedure entailed too many legal risks to justify its execution. Specifically, they advised, if a person should be caught breaking into one of the charity boxes, this could give rise to charges of entrapment. The risk was avoided in the field laboratory, because we had total control over the environment in which the antisocial act was performed, and we clearly were not going to press charges or report the act.

There was a major part of the study that was not included in the original proposal. This was the telephone call variable. Sometime after submitting the original proposal, but before the stimulus program was written, it seemed desirable to include a potentially very sensitive measure of antisocial imitation in the study, even if the level of violence it entailed was slight; Experiment VII (the telephone study) incorporates this notion.

The crux of the investigation, on the side of the dependent variable, is the action taken by subjects against a charity display. Therefore, the nature of the display was of extreme importance in the design of the study. One possibility was to create displays for fictitious, though familiar sounding charities; but the optimal solution was to make use of an existing charitable organization. We were fortunate to gain the cooperation of a nationally known charity, Project Hope. The cooperation of Project Hope in the study contributed enormously to its verisimilitude. Moreover, there was an added benefit: Project Hope was a medical charity. Thus, if stimulus similarity were a factor in stimulating imitation of the antisocial act, there could be no better choice.

This project was funded by a grant from CBS, Inc. to the Research Foundation of The City University of New York, and I served as principal investigator. Some may wonder whether a project so financed can truly be impartial. These readers are referred to the original research proposal appended to this study, for it defines the investigator's relationship to the funding source. (Appendix II). My experience was that the staff at CBS exhibited an attitude of cooperation, and total respect for my integrity as a scientist. And I commend them for this.

APPENDIX II

THE ORIGINAL RESEARCH PROPOSAL

THE EFFECT OF TELEVISION VIOLENCE ON THE
INCIDENCE OF VIOLENT ACTS IN THE COMMUNITY:
FIELD EXPERIMENTS

Stanley Milgram, Ph.D.
April 23, 1969

INTRODUCTION

Does television violence serve as a model that stimulates the production of violent acts in the community? The question is difficult
to answer using objective methods of assessment, but it is not impossible to answer given minimum control by the investigator of the
content of television programming. The basic idea of this proposal
is to determine whether the specific content of a television program
has a measurable effect on the incidence of violence in the community. The design of the experiment requires the cooperation of a
television network to the extent of preparing and broadcasting
a basic half hour program with several alternative endings. The
central character depicted in the program is confronted with a
moral dilemma. In the climax of one version of the program he

resolves the dilemma by performing a violent antisocial act. In the second version of the program, in which only the climax is altered, the central character does not perform the antisocial act, but provides a model of moral restraint. These two versions will be broadcast as ordinary television programs in different communities, and assessment will be made on the effects of the programs on the actual actions of persons in the respective communities.

BACKGROUND AND THEORY

As the relevant theoretical issues and experimental research were reviewed at the conference of social scientists convened on March 29 by the CBS Office of Social Research, they need not be repeated here at length. The formulations and research of Bandura and Walters (1963) on the modeling of aggressive actions in children, and the experimental studies of Berkowitz (1962) on the consequences of viewing aggressive actions in the laboratory are of interest. But they are not directly applicable to the question posed here for they do not deal with the effects of viewing television in naturalistic circumstances, and their measures of "violence" do not correspond to socially significant meanings of this term. What is needed is a means of testing whether violence on television that is viewed under ordinary circumstances serves to stimulate the commission of antisocial actions by those exposed to the television model.

FURTHER REQUIREMENTS OF A STUDY

If the televised violence is to have an effect that is measurable, a very specific form of antisocial action must be depicted; the reasons for this specificity will become clear later. Moreover, field experiments will have to be employed to test the effect of modeling of this action in the community. The idea in the present study is that the viewer in real life comes to be presented with a set of temptations identical to those confronted by the central character in a television drama. The question is whether exposure to one or another resolution by the television character influences the real life behavior of viewers. The action in question, if it is to address itself to socially meaningful issues, must contain an element of real violence. However, the violent action must be carefully tailored so that: (a) the community at large does not actually suffer even if imitation occurs; (b) a clear linkage can be shown between the television program and action in the community; and (c) the action under question is nontrivial. These are the indispensable requirements of a field experimental approach.

THE STIMULUS PROGRAM

Since the design of this research is closely tied to the specific television program that will serve as the violence inducing stimulus, let us consider a possible scenario for such a program, along with its alternative endings. This is intended not as a definitive outline of such a program, but only as an example of the general type of program that is required:

Possible scenario: The central character is a poor teenager. He is seen discussing his financial problems with the owner of a candy store. In the midst of the discussion a representative of a national charity enters, and requests permission to place a collection display for the charity just outside the candy store. The display consists of a distinctive porcelain bank on a stand. Money can be deposited in the slot of the bank. A sign appeals for contributions to the charity. The proprietor permits the official to place the display outside his store. Before departing, the charity representative asks whether the bank will be safe from vandals. The proprietor answers that the people in the neighborhood are poor, but that they have the dignity not to steal from children or charity. Occasional pedestrians are seen to drop coins in the bank.

The need for money becomes more critical for the central character. He meets a neighborhood girl, and invites her to an evening on the town. She agrees. He becomes painfully aware that he does not have the money for the date.

Alternative Sequences

Antisocial violence: After much inner conflict, and perhaps prodding by his peers, the central character approaches the candy

store at night, and employing a hammer smashes the charity display,
running off with its contents.

Positive social model: Same as above except that as he approaches
the charity display the central character remembers the comment
of the candy store owner about dignity, etc. After inner reflection
he puts the hammer away, takes some coins from his pocket, in-
serts them in the bank, and departs.

Two other variables can be incorporated into the design of the
program. The first concerns the consequences of the central character's actions (whether he is subsequently rewarded or punished);
the second is the degree of legitimation for his actions (e.g., his
mother needs the money for the purchase of eyeglasses, so that
she can retain her job as an embroiderer). These themes could
be inserted as brief alternative sequences, but for the moment,
let us focus on the principle issue, which concerns the modeling
of violence.

EFFECT OF THE PROGRAM
ON VIOLENCE IN THE COMMUNITY

How shall we assess the effects of the television program on
the community that has been exposed to it? Instead of attempting
to measure an increase in all possible forms of violence, muggings,
general assaults on property, actions against agents of law enforce-
ment, etc., this study focuses on the form of violence most likely,
because of cue similarity, to be directly stimulated by the television
program, that is, direct imitation of the central character's assault
on a specific charity display. A few days prior to the appearance
of the program in a community, there will appear in various loca-
tions porcelain charity displays of the type used in the program.
The figurines will be stationary, and thus cannot be carried away,
but they will be made of highly frangible materials. In order to
take the money from them, they must be smashed. (The figurines
will be set up by the investigator for the purposes of this study.)
The principal dependent measure is the ratio of figurines that
have been destroyed in communities that have been provided with
positive versus negative television models for this action. The

latency period following exposure to the program provides a second measure. Figurine placement will be such that it is unlikely that any one person will come across more than one figurine. Placement will be balanced in terms of neighborhoods and in terms of the degree of public scrutiny of the figurines. (Obviously, figurines in remote locales will be more readily assaulted than those continually in public view. On the other hand, the more people who see the figurines, the greater the likelihood that a potential assailant will notice it.) Permission to place the figurines will be negotiated with responsible city authorities, and in general this would mean the Office of the Mayor or City Manager in each of the communities studied. Placements would be on city owned property such as sidewalks, parking lots, etc. My past experience has been that city officials are generally cooperative in such matters when the true purposes of the study are revealed to them and the proper credentials of the investigator are established.

DEMOGRAPHIC ANALYSIS

The procedure permits the analysis of results in terms of a number of relevant demographic factors. The nature of the neighborhoods in which the figurines are placed will be carefully planned and results for neighborhoods of different class composition will be assessed. It is conceivable, for example, that television depiction of violence has effect only in lower class neighborhoods, where the threshold for violence is lower, and fewer restraints on aggression regulate the normal social behavior of participants.

The relatively anomic conditions of larger cities may lead to a higher amount of destruction than in small towns. Possibly, the cumulative effect of television violence can be examined in some fashion by studying communities in which the degree of television saturation varies. *Premeasure:* It is desirable to obtain a premeasure on figurine assaults in each community a fixed interval of time prior to the appearance of the television program. This would provide a base line for assessing the exact impact of the television program. It is conceivable, for example, that the positive social model will reduce destruction relative to the pretest base line.

FURTHER NOTE ON THE STIMULUS PROGRAM

The program is to be within the usual bounds of television fare, both in regard to its entertainment value, and the degree to which it depicts violence. It could be an ad hoc program, or to follow through an idea of Dr. Joseph Klapper, it could be embedded within an ongoing series. The advantages of placing the program in an ongoing series are:

1. It would cut production costs for the program.
2. It would in no way be conspicuously different from the expected television fare.
3. It would have a regular time slot and no complicated arrangements would be needed for time placement.

However, it would of necessity have to be an *extra* program within the series, that is, available as a substitute at particular stations whenever appropriate in terms of our experimental preparations. Substitution would be effected on different dates in different communities, as we were ready to study each. It would also, in this way, require only the minimal cooperation of the affiliate stations, since they would still be carrying the usual series in the normal time slot. The only requirement is that the affiliates (or major stations) substitute this particular number in the series at an agreed upon date.

LIMITATIONS OF THE STUDY

Although the study is designed to examine the effects of a specific instance of antisocial modeling, it does not in any direct way study the effects of the cumulative impact of television. Moreover, an outcome demonstrating a positive relationship between television violence and violence in real life is somewhat more convincing than the absence of such a finding, since it is always possible to say that extraneous variables swamped the experimental effects.

Another limitation is that the study does not deal with violence in its most extreme forms, that is, violence directed against a person. I see of no way that violence against a person can be legitimately employed as a dependent variable in this study, and the techniques described here are probably as far as one can go in field research. However, the destruction of a charity display in public places clearly falls within the definition of "violence against property" and is by no means of small social significance.

STUDY II

Study II is also a field experiment in which the independent variable is the television content of a specific program manufactured for the purpose of the experiment. It differs from Study I in one essential particular: namely, it eliminates unwanted variance by including in the experimental group only those persons who are known to have seen the program in question. This can be determined in two ways:

> 1. Listener determination of those who are watching by general telephone inquiry immediately after program.
> 2. A write-in free offer is made as a means of compiling a list of viewers. A large pool of names and addresses of those who viewed the program is obtained, and sampling from this pool is undertaken.

The basic approach is similar to that in Study I, and the identical television program is used. The chief difference is that in the present study the basic comparison is between experimental and control groups within a single community. Only persons known to have watched the television program are assigned to the experimental group, while persons who have not seen the program comprise the control group. (An additional refinement of this design is discussed later, under the heading Study IIb.) Experimental and control subjects are exposed to the figurine and a comparison of the destruction rates generated by each group constitutes the principal experimental datum. The technical difficulty is that of limiting exposure of the figurine to the predesignated groups. The technique for achieving this is as follows:

> a. A list of known viewers of the program and persons known not to have seen the program is compiled.

> b. Experimental and control subjects are brought into contact with the charity figurine. This is achieved by

scheduling subjects to appear in a physical location where they, and only they, will have contact with the figurine.

c. There are many ways to bring this about. For example, persons could be informed they have won a lottery and may pick up their gift, a transistor radio, at a specific office address. They will each be given the promised gift, but the critical fact is that they will be brought into contact with the figurine at that location.

d. The investigator will rent office space in a commercial building, the address where the lottery awards are to be distributed. The space will be carefully selected so that persons coming to the office and only such persons will encounter the charity appeal. The figurine will be placed in a location where it is relatively simple to steal or destroy without being seen. (See Milgram, 1965 for use of commercial office buildings in field experimentation.)

e. Since the figurine is under continuous scrutiny, it is possible to measure not only actual destruction, but movement in that direction (for example, attempts by any subject to tamper with the figurine). A relatively large number of subjects can be run and assigned to predetermined variations of the assessment situation (see later in this appendix).

Obviously, the scheduling of subjects, providing the proper rationale for bringing them to the office building, etc., need to be worked out in great detail. This study is more sensitive than Study I because it deals explicitly with persons known to have seen or not seen the television program. The technique permits the introduction of several experimental variations, for example, the possibility of raising the frustration or anger level of persons who come to the office building. Relevant demographic information and personal characteristics of subjects may be obtained easily. This would provide an opportunity to determine which types of viewers seem most affected by television violence, and which are not (assuming there is any effect at all).

The chief technical difficulty is likely to be a low destruction rate of figurines for both treatment conditions, even when figurines are optimally placed for destruction. A low destruction rate is, of course, of paramount interest in its own right and cannot be disregarded as an outcome. But for certain experimental purposes it may be useful to raise the destruction rate across both experimental and control conditions. A variety of means can be employed.

> a. Increase the attractiveness of the contents of the figurines, e.g., allow bills of large denomination to show through semitransparent walls of the bank.
>
> b. Further stimulate antisocial action by use of a live model. In this case two figurines are present. The naive subject observes a live model smash one and depart with its contents. The model remarks: "I seen someone doing this on television. There's plenty in this here one for me, bud. You can have the other one."

The live negative model would assuredly raise the destruction rates overall. The critical question, however, is whether the negative model would interact with viewing experience to generate *differential* destruction rates for experimental versus control groups. If this occurred, we would have to say that television viewing, in conjunction with other influences, increases the potential to antisocial violence. This is likely to be the most single sensitive test of the effects of television depicted violence of any discussed thus far. It also gets us beyond the simple minded notion that what is seen on television directly stimulates action, but takes account of the fact that television may interact with more proximal social influences to determine action in the person.

STUDY IIB

Study IIb represents a refinement in experimental design of Study II. If the practical details allowing for Study IIb can be arranged, it will be substituted for Study II. The optimal experimental design is to be found in a situation in which random segments of the population within a single community are simultaneously exposed to treatments A (negative television model), B (positive television model), and C (absence of television model). Persons drawn from each treatment condition are then individually exposed to the figurine at a single location as described under the details of Study II. The technical question is: How can different treatment conditions be simultaneously achieved on a physically proximal population?

The best solution requires the cooperation of two stations in a community. The program is shown on two stations simultaneously, one version on each station. A certain segment of the community is therefore exposed to treatment A and a certain segment to treatment B. To compile a list of persons viewing each version, an identical free offer is made on each program, differing only in P.O. Box to which requests are to be sent. (For example, in New York City, an offer could be made to send a free map of bus routes to persons who write in for it.) Once lists are compiled for each version, the procedures used in Study II are followed. Note that, using this procedure, it is not possible for one person to be exposed to both treatments (barring some very adroit channel switching or discussion of the program with others, an unlikely event).

The program need not be shown in prime time. Late evening viewing (after midnight) is acceptable so long as each version generates a list of a few thousand viewers. We need not worry about what fraction of the total community is exposed to the treatments, as is the case in Study I. For we need only sufficient numbers to fill the cells of the experimental design. There are no extraneous persons exposed to the figurine whose action could wash out differences otherwise attributable to the different treatment conditions.

MAGNITUDE OF THE STUDY

Study I, which requires the use of a separate community for each treatment condition, will be carried out in three to six cities in the course of a 30 month period. In Study II, approximately a thousand subjects will be individually studied in the experimental test situation, to be apportioned among the several experimental conditions already described.

INVESTIGATOR STATUS AND RIGHTS

The investigator reserves the right to modify the study in mid-course in the interest of better investigatory methods, though the principle point of focus will be the use of the content of television programs as the stimulus to antisocial behavior in the community. Major modifications of design will be communicated to the funding agency, but the investigator must be left free to introduce whatever technical modifications are required as the study develops. All employees on the research will be directly responsible to the investigator. The results of the investigation may be freely publicized by the investigator in forms and journals deemed suitable to him. Funding must be guaranteed at the outset for the total 30 month period of the investigation and cannot be withdrawn at midcourse, irrespective of the direction or trends of the findings. Since the source of funds for the investigation is a television network, and thus an interested party to the outcome, it is particularly important that the status of the investigator be clearly defined: he must function as an independent scientist whose judgments are to be completely his own and who will communicate the results of his investigation irrespective of their effects, negative or positive, for the funding source.

RESPONSIBILITY OF CBS

CBS will be responsible for the production of the experimental programs at no cost to the investigator, and according to the needs of the experimental design. CBS will use its good offices to encourage affiliates to show the program on dates appropriate to the needs of the investigation.

RESPONSIBILITY OF THE INVESTIGATOR

The investigator is responsible for all other aspects of the investigation: determination of relevant communities, procurement of materials needed for the study, negotiation with city officials, hiring of personnel, analysis of results, and preparation of reports of the study.

APPENDIX III

MODELING SCRIPTS

Appendix III contains the scripts of the three episodes of *Medical Center* created for the purposes of this experiment. The scripts are copyrighted and remain the property of Metro-Goldwyn-Mayer Inc. ("MGM") and are reprinted here through the courtesy of MGM. *Medical Center* is an Alfra Production in Association with M-G-M TV, a division of MGM. Frank Glicksman is the executive producer; Al C. Ward is the producer, and Don Brinkley the writer of the "Countdown" episodes. We begin with the first version of the story, in which Tom performs antisocial acts, and is subsequently punished.

ANTISOCIAL BEHAVIOR, WITH PUNISHMENT

We begin with the first version of the story, in which Tom performs antisocial acts, and is subsequently punished. The entire script follows:

MEDICAL CENTER

"COUNTDOWN"[1]

CAST

DR. JOE GANNON
DR. PAUL LOCHNER
NURSE CHAMBERS
TOM DESMOND
JULIE DESMOND
MR. CIAVELLI (and kids)
CHARLIE
WILLOUGHBY
MRS. KELLER
ORDERLY
BARTENDER
GLORIA
CASHIER (female)
TELETHON ANNOUNCER

SETS

INTERIORS:
  HOSPITAL ROOM
  GANNON'S OFFICE
  LOCHNER'S OFFICE
  EXAMINING ROOM
  WAITING ROOM
  WARD CORRIDOR
  AUDITORIUM
  HOSPITAL CORRIDOR
  STUDENT BOOK STORE
  WATERFRONT BAR
  TREATMENT ROOM
  CAFE
  CHARLIE'S ROOM
  CLEANING SHOP

EXTERIORS:
  MEDICAL CENTER
  HARBOR AREA
  STUDENT BOOK STORE
  BOAT YARD
  WATERFRONT BAR
  DRAMA AUDITORIUM

[1]A teleplay by Don Brinkley upon which a MEDICAL CENTER television series episode entitled "Countdown" was produced © Metro-Goldwyn-Mayer Inc. MCMLXX.

TEASER

FADE IN:
INT. EXAMINING ROOM—CLOSE ANGLE—NIGHT

On JULIE DESMOND, standing on a scale, wearing a hospital gown
and an anxious expression. She's 21; pretty; a bit too frail and
thin. Her strongest feature is her bright, valiant smile—which is
not in evidence now. PULL BACK to include DR. PAUL LOCHNER,
adjusting the weights. He reads the scale, doesn't like what he sees.

LOCHNER

You've lost three more pounds. How'd you manage that?

JULIE (ruefully)

Just lucky, I guess.

He gestures for her to step off the scale. She does. Frowning,
he makes some notes in her chart.

LOCHNER

Been taking your medication?
  (she nods)
*But you **haven't** been getting the rest you need.*

JULIE

*I've been trying, Doctor, really. But taking care of the apartment,
the baby—everything.*
  (helpless gesture)

LOCHNER

Isn't there anyone who can help you?

JULIE

*Just Tom. But the poor guy works here all night and on the boat
all day. I can't expect him to do **my** work too.*

LOCHNER

*All right, Julie, get dressed. The reports on your tests should be
ready in the morning . . .*

Lochner exits. HOLD ON Julie, concerned, then she reaches for
her clothes.

INT. WARD CORRIDOR—NIGHT

GANNON gets out of the elevator, sees Lochner.

> GANNON
>
> *Hello, Paul.*

> LOCHNER
>
> *Don't you ever go home?*

> GANNON
>
> *Well, you'll find out about it sooner or later—I have this penthouse on top of Four West—*
> (confidential)
> *—but I'll tell you, Paul—the orchestra plays too loud, the dancing girls get out of step—*

> LOCHNER (laughs)
>
> *All this rich life's boring me, too. So now that I've finished with Julie Desmond, I think I'll also call it a day.*

> GANNON (to business)
>
> *How is she?*

> LOCHNER (wearily)
>
> *I dunno. We think we have all the answers—until a case like Julie's comes along. Then we start playing guessing games.*
> (pause)
> *See you tomorrow?*

> GANNON
>
> *Why not. I need the experience.*

Lochner smiles and walks off. Gannon starts down the hall, the CAMERA TRACKING WITH him. Then Julie comes out of the Examination Room.

> JULIE
>
> *Oh, Doctor Gannon——*

> GANNON
>
> *Hello, Julie. How are you?*

                              JULIE
A lot better than Doctor Lochner thinks I am—
   (then)
Did Tom get to work on time today?

                              GANNON
As far as I know–Why?

                         P.A. VOICE (O.S.);
   (filtered)
Doctor Gannon–Doctor Joseph Gannon——

                              GANNON
He-ere we go again . . .

ZOOM IN CLOSE ON the wall-speaker, as:

                           P.A. VOICE
Stat, Four West. Doctor Gannon—stat, Four West . . .

CUT TO:
INT. HOSPITAL ROOM—CLOSE ANGLE—NIGHT

An OLD MAN, very ill, thrashing in bed, gasping desperately
for breath. PULL BACK to include NURSE MARSH, struggling
to control the frantic patient. His flailing arm (with IV tube
attached) yanks the IV standard over. Marsh manages to grab
the standard before it falls—but the glucose bottle hits the
floor and SHATTERS. Struggling with the patient, the IV,
Marsh calls into the corridor:

                              MARSH
Tom . . . !
   (no response)
Tom——!

Gannon hurries into the room, takes over, with:

                              GANNON
Get the I.P.P.B.—hurry!

INT. WARD CORIDOR—MARSH—NIGHT

rushes out of the room, looks up and down the hall.

MARSH
Tom . . . !

No response. Infuriated, she hurries down the hall.

INT. TREATMENT ROOM—TOM DESMOND—NIGHT

slumped in one chair, feet propped on another——sound asleep.
He's about 22–23, wears the whites of an orderly; rough-hewn
good looks, with the taut, driven quality of a young man who's
had to work too hard for too little. Now the door bursts open
and Marsh enters. Tom pops awake, rises groggily, as:

CHAMBERS
*Well now, isn't that cozy! Sorry to disturb your beauty rest, but
a man's dying out there . . . !*

TOM (flustered)
I'm——sorry, Miss Chambers, I——

But she has pushed past him, grabbed the breathing machine,
and rushed out again. HOLD ON Tom——confused, contrite. A
moment, then he steps out into the corridor.

INT. WARD CORRIDOR—FAVORING CHAMBERS—NIGHT

wheels the machine to the old man's room. Tom appears behind
her.

TOM (calls)
Miss Chambers—I'm sorry—can I do anything——?

CHAMBERS
Yes—do your sleeping on your own time!

She enters the room, kicks the door shut.

ANGLE—TOM

feeling useless, ashamed. His weariness is compounded by his
guilt. TRACK WITH him to a nearby laundry cart. He wheels it
dispiritedly to a closet near the elevators. He starts transferring
the clean laundry from cart to shelves. The elevator doors open.

Another ORDERLY wheels a dolly off the elevator. It contains a few large cartons. Tom watches as the Orderly dips into a carton, takes out a "donation box," and a placard, places the display on the Ward Desk.

                         TOM
   *What's **that**?*

CLOSE ANGLE—THE DISPLAY

The donation-box is a model of the new clinic building, in transparent plastic, with a slot for depositing money. The accompanying placard reads:

> *HELP YOURSELF TO BETTER HEALTH!*
> *GIVE NOW TO YOUR NEW*
> *COMMUNITY CLINIC*

PULL BACK to include the Orderly. Tom joins him, as:

                      ORDERLY
   For the new clinic. They're putting them all over town.

                         TOM
   Give—give—everybody's got his hand out.

Tom gives him a disgusted look, returns to the laundry. To demonstrate his righteousness, the Orderly deposits a coin in the empty container, and wheels the dolly O.S.

INT. HOSPITAL ROOM—FAVORING GANNON—NIGHT

The old man is breathing easily now; the I.P.P.B. is hooked up. Gannon addresses Chambers.

                       GANNON
   Keep a close eye on him. And order special nurses.

                      CHAMBERS
   Yes sir.

Gannon exits.

INT. WARD CORRIDOR—FAVORING TOM—NIGHT

Seeing Gannon approaching, he hurries to empty the cart and push it away. But:

GANNON

Tom . . .

TOM

I'm—sorry about falling asleep, Doctor Gannon. Guess I've been pushing myself a little too hard . . .

GANNON

If the patient had died, that wouldn't have been much of an excuse.

TOM (tired; edgy)

Look, I said I'm sorry. What else can I do?

GANNON

*You can start getting your sleep at **home**. Tom, I know it's rough holding down two jobs—I've done it myself—but we can't jeopardize our patients because of your——*

TOM (defensive)

Man, you sure can lean on a guy! You've been on my back ever since you gave me this crummy job . . .

GANNON (quietly)

That's not true, and you know it. All I expect of you is——

TOM (heatedly)

*Yeah, I know what you expect! Give a guy a hand-out and you expect him to lick your fingers. Well, I don't need the work **that** bad. Go get yourself another boy.*

ANGLE—FAVORING GANNON

A moment. What can he do? As he turns away, Marsh joins him. She notices the laundry cart.

MARSH

Where's Tom?

GANNON

He just quit.

MARSH

Quit . . . ? He can't afford to do that . . .

GANNON

And we can't afford to be shorthanded. Tell them to hire another orderly.

EXT. MEDICAL CENTER—FULL SHOT—NIGHT

Tom comes out of the building, still accelerated by his anger. But as he starts away, reality closes in on him. He moves into F.G., pauses, halted by second thoughts. He turns, looks back at the building. Should he, or shouldn't he? He makes his decision: the hell with it! Defiantly, he walks away from the Medical Center.

FADE OUT.

END TEASER

ACT ONE

FADE IN:
EXT. HARBOR AREA—FULL SHOT—DAY

to ESTABLISH.

ANGLE—AT TOM'S BOAT SLIP

A small, battered fishing boat is tied in the slip. "The Julie I." It contains assorted fishing gear, diving equipment, deisel drums, towing lines, etc. A hand-lettered sign on the slip announces:

> *BOAT FOR HIRE*
> *NO JOB TOO SMALL*
> *TOM DESMOND*

Tom is working on the tired engine. He doesn't see CHARLIE ——about 50, a gentle waterfront hustler—until:

> CHARLIE
> *How's it going, Tom?*

> TOM
> *Fine, fine . . . Lining up some good prospects.*

> CHARLIE
> *Oh—just prospects again—Sounds like another late payment. Tom, I don't want to have to repossess this old tub.*

Tom tosses his tools aside, hops on the slip, wiping his hands with a rag, as:

> TOM
> *Come o-on, Charlie, you know how my luck's been running. Julie's been sick . . . and the harbor's been dead lately. Soon as the fishing season begins, I'll have all the work I can handle . . .*

> CHARLIE
> *I can't wait that long, kid. I got bills to pay too. Can't you give me **one** payment, even?*

Julie Desmond can be seen approaching in B.G., as:

> TOM
>
> *Look, you've waited* **this** *long. Another two, three days won't make any difference . . .*

> JULIE
>
> *Hi, darling . . . ! Morning, Charlie.*

> CHARLIE
>
> *Morning, Julie.*

> TOM (surprised)
>
> *Hey, what're you doing here?*

> JULIE
>
> *Any reason why I can't come down to see my husband?*

> CHARLIE
>
> *Julie . . .*

She runs into Tom's arms. Their kiss is long, loving, ardent. Charlie fidgets self-consciously. When they finally break:

> CHARLIE
>
> *Okay, Tom. See you in two, three days.* **No later.**

> TOM
>
> *Thanks, Charlie.*

ANGLE—FAVORING JULIE

> JULIE (gazing after Charlie)
>
> *Troubles?*

> TOM
>
> *Same old thing.*

> JULIE
>
> *Tom, I've been worried sick about you. I called the hospital last night. They said you weren't there.*

> TOM (guiltily)
>
> *Yeah . . . I——got off early . . .*

> JULIE
>
> *Why didn't you come home?*

> TOM
>
> *Well, I—had to get this engine working again, and——*
> (changes subject)
> *Hey, who's watching the baby? You didn't leave her with your mother . . . !*

> JULIE (smiles)
>
> *No, love, she's with Mrs. Ciavelli.*

> TOM
>
> *Are you telling me the truth?*

> JULIE (wearily)
>
> *Yes. And I wish you'd stop being so paranoiac about my parents. They really aren't that bad, y'know.*

> TOM
>
> *No, but they think **I** am . . .*
> (with an edge)
> *After all, I never made it to college like their daughter. I just got as far as Juvenile Hall.*

> JULIE
>
> *Tom, don't talk that way!*

> TOM
>
> *Okay, okay, let's not argue . . .*

He hops into the boat to resume his work. Julie fidgets uneasily for a moment. Finally:

> JULIE (reluctantly)
>
> *Hey, Mr. Desmond—what **really** happened to you last night?*

ANGLE—FAVORING TOM

He stiffens. Then, realizing he can't lie to her:

> TOM
>
> *Well, if you must know, I got into a hassle with Doctor Gannon —and quit my job.*

> JULIE
>
> *Oh, Tom . . .*

TOM
I had to, Julie. He was really riding me.

JULIE
*But honey, he **is** the one who gave you the job.*

TOM
Yeah, as a favor to you. I may not have anything else, but I do have some pride.

JULIE (softens)
Well—I—I'd rather have you home nights anyway.

TOM (grins, kisses her)
Yeah, that does have certain advantages—I'll find another job, though—just till things pick up around here.

ANGLE—FAVORING JULIE

JULIE
I've got a better idea. My old job at the book store is still open. I could——

TOM
Nothing doing. You've been told to rest, to stay off your feet . . .

JULIE (still trying)
Tell you what: I'm seeing Doctor Lochner this morning. The report on my five-thousand-mile check-up. I'll ask him if I'm well enough to work. Even part-time would help . . .

TOM
When's your appointment?

JULIE
Eleven o'clock.

TOM (a beat, then)
C'mon, I'll go with you . . .

CUT TO:

INT. CONFERENCE ROOM—CLOSE ANGLE—DAY

A donation-box display on the Board table. PULL BACK to

include Lochner, referring to the display as he speaks. He's addressing 5 or 6 other DOCTORS, including Gannon.

> LOCHNER
>
> *—so, gentlemen, the campaign is now in high gear . . . these donation-boxes have been placed all over the city—we've arranged for radio, TV, and newspaper interviews—a big telethon is scheduled for next week. Joe, here, is handling the details. Any help you can give him would be gratefully appreciated.*
> (then)
> *Any questions?*
> (then)
> *All right, gentlemen, thanks for your time . . .*

The meeting adjourns. The doctors file out. Gannon, however, approaches Lochner with:

> GANNON
>
> *Paul, we need a speaker at that fund-raising dinner tomorrow night for the faculty auxiliary. The vice-chancellor can't make it.*

> LOCHNER (grimaces)
>
> *Ah, those dinners. Frozen-faced clubwomen and chicken a la king . . .*

> GANNON
>
> *No such luxury for this one. It's tuna casserole. All that for ten minutes of sparkling oratory.*

A KNOCK at the door. They turn toward it.

ANGLE—TOWARD THE DOOR

Tom stands in the open doorway, looking uneasy.

> TOM
>
> *'Scuse me, Doctor Gannon. They——told me I'd find you here . . .*

> GANNON
>
> *Come on in, Tom . . .*

LOCHNER

I'm leaving anyway . . .
  (looks at watch)
Matter of fact, I have a date with your wife.

TOM

Yes sir. She's waiting downstairs.

Lochner exits. Gannon waits for Tom to speak. Finally:

TOM (with difficulty)

I——want to apologize for last night. I was wrong. I——had no right to walk out like that.

GANNON

Forget it.

TOM (rueful smile)

I need the work. When you've done a couple of hitches in Juvie Hall like me, jobs are hard to get.

GANNON

I'm aware of that, Tom. You can come back to work here as soon as there's another opening.

TOM (slow take)

Another opening? What's the matter with the one I had?

GANNON

It was filled this morning. I'm sorry, Tom, I——

TOM

*Look, I **need** that job. I've got a sick wife, a six-month-old baby, a thousand debts——*

ANGLE—FAVORING GANNON

GANNON

Tom, I'm sorry. I really am. I didn't think you'd be coming back.

TOM (bitterly)

Sure—

He turns away, sees the donation-box display on the table.

TOM (cont'd, scornfully)
*You guys give away millions in free medical care, food, clothes—
to any sad-eyed moocher with his hand out. But when a guy wants
to* **work** *for his bread, you slam the door in his face!*

GANNON
*The door's wide open, Tom. To you and anyone else. You want
another chance, get in line.*

TOM
Thanks—thanks a lot.

Tom glares at him a moment, slams the display on the table,
and marches out.

CUT TO:
INT. LOCHNER'S OFFICE—
FAVORING LOCHNER—DAY

at his desk, riffling through reports. Julie is seated opposite him,
as:

LOCHNER
A job?? Julie, you know better than that . . .

JULIE
*Just a few hours a day—at the Student Book Store. I used to work
there before I left school.*

LOCHNER
*Afraid not, Julie. These tests aren't as encouraging as I'd like
them to be . . .*
   (then)
We'll have to continue the bed-rest and regular doses of cortisone.

ANGLE—FAVORING JULIE

JULIE
*Bed-rest! I've had to quit school, quit my job—and now I'm
studying to be a vegetable. Am I going to have this stupid disease
all my life?*

LOCHNER
Depends on how you treat it.

>   JULIE (glumly)
> *Treat it! I can't even **pronounce** it.*
>
>   LOCHNER
> *"Polyarteritis nodosa."*
>
>   JULIE
> *Why can't they give it a simple name—like Fred—or Irving?*
>
>   LOCHNER
> *Because there's nothing simple about it. It causes an inflamma-*
> *tion of your blood vessels—and that creates all kinds of problems.*
> *Now, do you want a recurrence of that attack you had a few weeks*
> *ago?*
>
>   JULIE
> *Oh, that couldn't happen again! I feel too healthy.*
>
>   LOCHNER
> *Then keep it that way. Go home, and go to bed. I'll see you next*
> *week. Same time.*

He starts to the door, but:

>   JULIE
> *Doctor Lochner . . . ?*
>   (he turns)
> *I——imagine you heard about Tom . . . ?*
>   (he nods)
> *He's much too proud to ask—but he really **needs** that job. Any*
> *chance of his getting it back?*
>
>   LOCHNER
> *Well, he's with Doctor Gannon right now.*
>
>   JULIE (delighted)
> *He is?? O-oh, that guy . . . !*

CUT TO:
EXT. MEDICAL CENTER—FAVORING TOM—DAY

seated on the steps outside the lobby, brooding. Julie rushes
out of the building, runs eagerly over to him. (*NOTE:* A
donation-box display is visible just inside the lobby doors.)

                   JULIE
You went to see Doctor Gannon!

                TOM (caught)
Uh—yeah—thought I'd let him know there were no hard feelings.

                   JULIE
I—I thought you might have gone to get your job back.

             TOM (false bravado)
*You kidding? You think I'd go crawling back to **him** for a——a——
lousy job like **that**??*

Julie studies him a moment, sensing the false bravado. Then:

                   JULIE
Well, I thought—if you wanted it bad enough . . .

                   TOM
I'll find something better . . .

                   JULIE
Tom, it's not that easy . . .

                   TOM
*You mean it's not that easy for **me**, right?*

                   JULIE
Tom, please.

              TOM (going on)
*I haven't been in trouble since I was seventeen—but nobody lets
me forget it. Not even you.*

                   JULIE
Oh, come o-on, you're not being fair . . . !

                   TOM
Being fair doesn't count anymore.

He takes her arm, escorts her down the stairs.

ANGLE—TRUCKING SHOT

They walk in silence, each lost in private thought. The conversation has stirred up some long-dormant doubts in Julie's mind.

At one point she steals a quick glance at her young husband. Then:

                              JULIE
*Hey, Mr. Desmond. Want some **good** news?*
   (he looks up)
Your wife is practically cured.

                    TOM (stops; stares)
You mean that . . . ?

                              JULIE
Ask Doctor Lochner. He gave me his whole-hearted permission to go out and get a job.

                              TOM
Julie, if you're lying to me——

                              JULIE
As long as I take my pills and come in for regular check-ups, I can work anyplace I want!

                    TOM (heartfelt)
He-ey, that's great . . . beautiful!
   (hugs her happily)
But look—I don't want you to work. I want you to stay home and take care of Tina——

                              JULIE
Just for a while, Tom, till you get started again. That way, we can pay off the boat and——

                              TOM
I still don't like it.

                              JULIE
Darling, we have to be realistic about this . . .

                    TOM (reluctantly)
Okay, okay—but the day I start work, I expect you to quit. Agreed?

                              JULIE
Right on!

She extends her hand. He shakes it. She moves into his arms, enjoying his embrace, oblivious to the world around them. A beat. Then they move away, arm in arm.

CUT TO:
INT. WARD CORRIDOR—ON MARSH—DAY

on the phone, her back to elevator as Gannon gets off, approaches.

> MARSH (into phone)
> *No sir, he's still in surgery.*
> (listens, then)
> *Yes sir. He'll be glad to hear that. Yes, I'll tell him.*

As she hangs up and makes a note of the call, a PATIENT in robe and slippers pauses at the desk to inspect the donation-box display. He takes a coin from his pocket, deposits it, and walks O.S.

> MARSH
> *Thank you.*

ANGLE—FAVORING GANNON

Marsh sees him as he goes behind the desk.

> MARSH
> *How'd it go?*

> GANNON (wearily)
> *Malignant. But I think we got it all. Any calls?*

> MARSH
> *The Chancellor's office. The Mayor's on campus today. He's given his official endorsement to the new clinic . . .*

> GANNON
> *Good . . .*
> (sudden thought)
> *Maybe I can talk him into appearing on the telethon. . .*

> MARSH
> *He's with the Chancellor now . . .*

GANNON (looks at watch)
I'd better get over there . . .

He starts away, notices the donation-box display. He picks it up, rattles it. It's about half-filled with coins.

GANNON (pleased)
All this in three days? We must be doing something right.

And he hurries away.

CUT TO:
EXT. MEDICAL CENTER—FULL SHOT—DAY

Through the doors, we see Gannon crossing the lobby, TOWARD CAMERA. He pauses at the donation-box inside the doors. It's more than half-filled. Pleased, he hurries out of the building, and away.

CUT TO:
EXT. STUDENT BOOK STORE—TO ESTABLISH—DAY

Just inside the open door, mounted like a gum-ball machine, is another donation-box display, moderately filled. Gannon strides INTO THE SHOT, does a take at the sight of the display, pauses to inspect it. This, too, pleases him. But as he starts on his way again, he notices something inside the store.

INT. STUDENT BOOK STORE—GANNON'S POV—DAY

Through the open door (or the display window), Julie Desmond can be seen. Carrying a stack of books, she vanishes behind some shelves.

EXT. STUDENT BOOK STORE—
BACK TO GANNON—DAY

surprised, concerned. He considers this a moment, decides to do something about it. He enters the store.

INT. STUDENT BOOK STORE—ANGLE—JULIE—DAY

Hidden behind the stacks, she moves into F.G., sets her books down, and tries to fight off a wave of nausea and pain. A bristling, agonizing moment. Finally it passes. Pulling herself together, she picks up the books and prepares to move along. But:

> GANNON'S VOICE (O.S.)
>
> *Hello, Julie . . .*

She turns, startled. ANGLE WIDENS to include Gannon as he approaches. Julie greets him uneasily, self-consciously.

> JULIE
>
> *Hi, Doctor Gannon. You——interested in some books . . . ?*

> GANNON
>
> *I'm more interested in you. How long have you been working here?*

> JULIE
>
> *A few days. Just filling in for someone. Part-time . . .*

> GANNON
>
> *Does Doctor Lochner know about it?*

> JULIE
>
> *Well, not exactly . . .*
>   (fearfully)
> *You won't tell him, will you? He'll make me quit—and—it's only temporary—just till Tom finds a job . . .*

ANGLE—FAVORING GANNON

> GANNON (studies her, concerned)
>
> *How old is your baby, Julie?*

> JULIE
>
> *Six months. Our neighbor is taking care of her——*

> GANNON
>
> *If you found the baby playing with a loaded gun, would you take it away from her or just ignore it?*

> JULIE (feeling trapped)
>
> *Doctor Gannon—what are you trying to do to us?? Why don't you just——just——**leave us alone**??*

GANNON (a beat)

All right, Julie. Sorry I interfered. But you are playing with a loaded gun.

He turns, and exits. HOLD ON Julie——shaken by the conversation. A moment, then she gathers up the books and moves to a nearby ladder.

EXT. STUDENT BOOK STORE—GANNON—DAY

strides out of the store, pauses——looks back thoughtfully. What to do? A moment, then he walks on.

INT. STUDENT BOOK STORE—ANGLE—JULIE—DAY

Behind the stacks, she climbs the ladder——carrying an armful of books for the upper shelves. Another wave of nausea engulfs her. She falters. Then the pain hits——and hard. She stifles a cry, doubles up in sudden agony. The books fly out of her hands. She loses her balance, and topples to the floor.

FADE OUT.

END ACT ONE

ACT TWO

FADE IN:
EXT. HARBOR AREA—AT TOM'S BOAT SLIP—DAY

Tom is on the boat, cleaning it up. The engine has been reassembled. Now he's gathering up his tools, tidying up the assorted equipment. He doesn't notice WILLOUGHBY approaching. He's a big, hearty, hard-grained man of 50, wearing coveralls and a woolen mariner's cap.

> WILLOUGHBY
> *Hey, son, where can I find Tom Desmond?*

> TOM
> *Right here.*

Tom climbs out of the boat, to the slip, as:

> WILLOUGHBY
> *Name's Willoughby. Willoughby Maritime Service . . .*
> (hands Tom a card)
> *Hear you've got a boat for hire.*

> TOM
> *Yes sir, I sure have.*

> WILLOUGHBY
> *We're starting a job, Monday. South end of the harbor. Need a utility boat for about two, three weeks.*

> TOM (eagerly)
> *Well, this one's available, Mr. Willoughby . . . I'll have her ready to go by Monday for sure.*

Willoughby takes a moment to look at the boat.

> WILLOUGHBY
> *Ain't exactly the Queen Mary, is she?*

> TOM
> *She gets the work done.*

> WILLOUGHBY (warily)
What about rates?

> TOM

Lowest on the water. Just getting started. Trying to build up my own business.
   (indicates boat sign)
See that, Mr. Willoughby—The Julie One—I plan to have Julie Two and right up the line.

Willoughby considers this a moment, decides he approves.

> WILLOUGHBY
All right, son. Stop by the office in an hour. We'll hash out the deal.

He turns abruptly, strides away. HOLD ON Tom, delighted.

> TOM
*Yes **sir**, I'll be there!*

TRUCK WITH him, on the run, to the nearby telephone booth. (*NOTE:* In harbor area, there are booths or pay phones at the foot of most slips.)

ANGLE—INTO THE PHONE BOOTH

Tom enters, leaves the door open. He deposits a coin, dials a number——eager, excited. Then:

> TOM (into phone)
Charlie? Tom Desmond. Got a shock for you: I'll have some of your money on Monday.

INT. CHARLIE'S ROOM—DAY

> CHARLIE (into phone)
Now look, Tom—if this is a stall—

INTERCUTTING WITH Tom.

> TOM (into phone)
Charlie, this isn't a stall. I'm working for Willoughby Maritime Service——

INTERCUT—A BATTERED STATION WAGON

stops nearby. At the wheel: MR. CIAVELLI, a harried-looking Italian family man. He walks off toward Tom's boat.

ANGLE—AT PHONE BOOTH—INTERCUTTING

> TOM (into phone)
> *I'm **not** stalling, Charlie! I'll be at Willoughby's office in an hour— you can see for yourself!*

> CHARLIE
> *You really **mean** Monday.*

> TOM
> *Right. Monday, for sure. Thanks again, Charlie.*

He hangs up, steps out of the booth. Ciavelli rushes up to him, with:

> CIAVELLI
> *Tom——*

> TOM (surprised)
> *Well, hi, Mr. Ciavelli. What——*

> CIAVELLI
> *Been looking all over for you——*

> TOM (realizing)
> *What's wrong? Anything happen to Tina? Is she——*

> CIAVELLI
> *No, no, the baby's fine. It's Julie—she's sick——*

> TOM
> *What do you mean, sick? What's happened——*

> CIAVELLI
> *The Medical Center—they called—it's an emergency—she got sick in the book store and——*

But Tom has already rushed away.

CUT TO:
INT. LOCHNER'S OFFICE—TOWARD THE DOOR—DAY

It opens. Lochner and Gannon enter, in heated debate. Lochner is carrying some fresh x-rays which he places on the view boxes, during:

LOCHNER

*. . . I still think we might get by treating it **medically**, Joe. With cortisone. It may only be the polyarteritis . . .*
(then)
Have you seen these x-rays?

GANNON

Yeah, they don't tell us a thing.
(then)
*Look, Paul, she's in severe pain. We can't be sure there hasn't been permanent damage to the small intestine. If there's dead tissue in there, it **has** to be removed!*

LOCHNER

If it's there. Suppose you open her up and discover you're wrong?

GANNON

*Suppose I'm right and the dead tissue **is** there? The risk of waiting may be more dangerous than the surgery.*

The PHONE RINGS. Lochner punches the intercom button, speaks into the phone.

LOCHNER

Yes?
(then)
Good. Send him in.
(hangs up)
Tom's here.

ANGLE—TOWARD THE DOOR

It opens. Tom enters——looking shaken, distraught.

LOCHNER

Come on in, Tom . . .

TOM

Just saw Julie. Man, she's having a miserable time . . .

LOCHNER (nods)
We've been trying to decide how we can best help her.

TOM (bitterly)
*Yeah, you've been a big help—telling her she could go back to work
. . .*

LOCHNER (surprised)
I told her . . .?

GANNON (quickly)
That was Julie's idea, Tom. Not Doctor Lochner's.

TOM
He gave her permission! She told me!

LOCHNER (quietly)
I'm afraid that's not true . . .

TOM
Now, why would she lie about a thing like that?

GANNON
*Maybe she was trying to ease the strain on you—till you found a
job.*

Tom stares at them helplessly. With a gesture of sheer frustration,
he flops into a chair.

TOM
Oh man, what a freaky wife I picked. What'm I gonna do with her?

GANNON
*That's what **we've** been discussing: what to do with Julie.*

ANGLE—FAVORING LOCHNER

LOCHNER
*It's possible surgery may be indicated. But we're hoping we can get
by without it.*

GANNON
*If there's been severe tissue damage, all the medicine in the world
won't help. The only way we can be sure is through exploratory surgery.*

> TOM
>
> *Well, if it's necessary . . .*

> LOCHNER
>
> *That's the point: it may **not** be necessary, and we'll do our best to avoid it. We'll try this treatment for a while. If there's no improvement, we'll have to operate.*

> TOM
>
> *She can't take much more of that pain. When will you know?*

> LOCHNER
>
> *Another few hours . . .*

> TOM
>
> *Well, I'll be here. I——*
> (suddenly)
> *Hey—wait—I'm supposed to see about a job . . .*
> (rises quickly)
> *I——better call that guy . . .*

And he hurries out.

INT. HOSPITAL CORRIDOR—TOM—DAY

TRUCK WITH him along the hall to the phone booth. He fishes in his pockets, finds the card Willoughby gave him. He enters the booth, deposits a coin, refers to the card as he dials the number. Then, into the phone:

> TOM
>
> *Hello? Mr. Willoughby, please.*

INT. WILLOUGHBY'S OFFICE—INTERCUT—DAY

> SECRETARY
>
> *He's not in. Who's calling?*

> TOM
>
> *This is Tom Desmond. I had an appointment with him about a job—but my wife got sick—they may have to operate. I'm at the Medical Center right now. It may be a few hours. Tell Mr. Willoughby I'll be there as soon as I can get away. Okay, thanks.*

He hangs up worried.

CUT TO:
INT. WARD CORRIDOR—CLOSE ANGLE—DAY

The closed door of a private room. Now it opens. Gannon comes out, wearing a white coat. TRUCK WITH him to where Tom is seated, on a bench in the hall. Tom sees him, rises apprehensively.

GANNON

She's in too much pain, Tom. The treatment's not working. We'd better not wait any longer.

TOM

Surgery . . .?
   (Gannon nods)
Can she handle it, Doc . . .?

GANNON

Well, she's young, with a lot to live for—and a strong desire to keep on living. I think she can handle it.

TOM (a beat)

May I see her . . .?

Gannon nods. Tom heads for the room.

CUT TO:
INT. HOSPITAL—A NURSE AND ORDERLY—DAY

They've just transferred Julie from her bed to a gurney. As they start to wheel her out, Tom enters the room. He takes Julie's hand, leans over, kisses her on the cheek.

ANGLE—FAVORING JULIE

Her eyes flutter open. She's heavily sedated.

JULIE

Tom . . .?

TOM

Right here, Julie.

JULIE

Is——Tina all right?

TOM

She's fine. She's with Mr. and Mrs. Ciavelli.

JULIE (weakly)
One of their kids had a runny nose. Don't let her catch cold, Tom.

TOM

I won't. I promise.

A moment. She reaches up, strokes his face gently.

JULIE
I'm sorry, darling. I—— I—— really goofed, didn't I . . .

TOM
No . . . you were trying to help . . .

JULIE
Some help. Flat on my back with needles in my arm . . .

TOM
Just get well, baby, okay?
    (then)
Listen, I——I've got a job, at the harbor. A good one. You'll have to get well fast so you can help me spend all our money. Agreed?

JULIE (smiles; extends her hand)
Right on!

He takes her hand, shakes it——and kisses it, as the gurney is wheeled away.

CUT TO:
INT. O.R.—FULL SHOT—DAY

Surgical procedure. They're well into the operation by now.

GANNON
Retractor . . .
    (then)
Hold this, will you, Paul?

Surgical procedure. Gannon looks in abdomen. Then:

> GANNON
Ah . . . there you are . . . look at that!

> LOCHNER (smiles)
You were right, Joe. Can you get it all?

> GANNON
I don't know.

CUT TO:

INT. WAITING ROOM—ANGLE—TOM—DAY

slumped in a chair, waiting. He stares at a donation-box display. He rises, stretches restlessly, notices the clock on the wall.

HIS POV—UP AT WALL CLOCK

It registers 4:50.

BACK TO TOM

He HEARS FOOTSTEPS approaching. PAN WITH him to the doorway. Gannon appears, looking tired, solemn.

> TOM
Well . . .?

> GANNON
There was some dead tissue there, all right. We removed it.

> TOM
And Julie? How is she?

> GANNON
She's doing very well. Hopefully, there won't be any problems.

> TOM (relieved)
Oh man, that's good news . . .!
> (then)
Can I see her?

ANGLE—FAVORING GANNON

GANNON
She's still in the Recovery Room. She'll be there at least another hour.

TOM (looks at wall clock)
Would I have time to go down to the harbor? I've got to see a man about a job.

GANNON (nods)
Take your time. Julie won't be in her room for a while yet.

TOM
Thanks, Doc. Thanks again . . .

He hurries away.

CUT TO:
EXT. BOAT YARD—CLOSE ANGLE—DAY

The gate in the high chain-like fence bears the sign:

**WILLOUGHBY
MARITIME
SERVICE, INC.**

Willoughby pulls the gate shut after him, takes a moment to clock the heavy padlock. PAN WITH him to his car, parked nearby. As he's about to get in, Tom comes racing toward him, preceded by:

TOM'S VOICE
Mr. Willoughby——!

Willoughby turns; Tom comes puffing up to him.

WILLOUGHBY
You're a bit late, son. About a half a day.

TOM
Didn't you get my message? My wife got sick—had an emergency operation. I got here as soon as I could . . .

WILLOUGHBY (unsure)
Well, I'm sorry to hear that. How's she doing.

> TOM

So far, so good. Look, I know it's late—but do you have time to talk . . .?

> WILLOUGHBY

About what?

> TOM

The job. Our contract . . .

> WILLOUGHBY

Son, that job's been taken.

> TOM (desperate)

*But you **knew** I wanted it!*

> WILLOUGHBY

Well, I figured with your wife being sick, you'd want to be with her . . . Anyway, it wasn't that big of a deal.

Tom glares at him, his private form of paranoia taking over again:

> TOM

You been talking to people about me, right?

> WILLOUGHBY

Well, sure, I asked around . . .

> TOM (bitterly)

Yeah, and I know what they told you. That's why you didn't hire me.

> WILLOUGHBY

Son, I don't have the slightest idea what you're talking about . . .
>   (gets into car)
> *Stop by in a few weeks. We may need another boat. My best to the little lady.*

He starts the car, drives away. HOLD ON Tom——stunned, lost. A long moment. He starts walking away, simmering with frustration. He kicks viciously at a stone, and keeps on walking——faster, faster.

CUT TO:
EXT. HARBOR AREA—TOM'S BOAT SLIP—DAY

Charlie is in the boat, starting the engine. He lets it idle while he hops up to the slip and casts off the lines. As he hops back into the boat:

TOM'S VOICE (O.S.)

Hey! Charlie—!!

HIS POV—TOM

running like hell toward the slip.

BACK TO CHARLIE

He'd hoped to avoid this. He puts the motor in gear and shoves off. The boat chugs slowly away from the slip——as Tom races INTO THE SHOT. He stands on the edge of the slip, calling:

TOM (cont'd)

Charlie—where you taking my boat?

CHARLIE

It'll be in my boat yard—till you pay your bills.

TOM

I told you—I've got a job——!

CHARLIE

Stow it, Tom! I called Willoughby this afternoon! He said you never showed up!

TOM (frantic)

*There's a reason, Charlie, I swear! Please—**you gotta listen to me! Please, Charlie . . .!***

But Charlie has the boat under way now, chugging down the channel.

ANGLE—TOM

alone on the empty slip——lost, helpless——watching his hopes drift away with the chugging "The Julie I".

FADE OUT.

END ACT TWO

ACT THREE

FADE IN:
INT. HOSPITAL ROOM—TOWARD THE DOOR—NIGHT

It opens. Gannon enters the dimly lighted room. PAN WITH him
to the bed, where Julie is dozing. She has an I.V. in her arm.
He lights the small lamp on the night table. Julie stirs, opens
her eyes.

JULIE (softly)

Tom . . .?

GANNON

Doctor Gannon, Julie.

JULIE (disappointed)

Oh. Hi . . .

GANNON

How're you feeling?

ANGLE—FAVORING JULIE

JULIE

Terrible, but I'm glad it's over.
  (then)
Has Tom been here?

GANNON

*He was here till you came out of surgery. When he knew you were
all right, he left for the harbor. Something about a new job.*

JULIE

When was that?

GANNON

About 5 o'clock.

JULIE

What time is it now?

GANNON
Almost seven. But there's nothing to be concerned about. They may have put him right to work.
(then)
Now, let's take a look at my embroidery . . .

As he prepares to examine her———

CUT TO:
INT. WARD CORRIDOR—AT THE
FIRE EXIT—NIGHT

The door opens, discharging Mr. Ciavelli and three of four of his kids. Ciavelli is now carrying a tiny baby in his arms. He gestures the kids over to a nearby bench, with:

CIAVELLI
*You wait right here, understand? No noise, no fighting. Everybody quiet and **nice**. You hear me?*

The kids nod solemnly. Ciavelli starts away, carrying the baby. The moment his back is turned, one boy yanks another one's hair. The second boy kicks the third one in the leg. Suddenly Ciavelli stops, turns back to look at them. Instantly they're little angels again. Satisfied, he moves O.S. The kids pick up where they left off.

ANGLE—AT WARD DESK

Ciavelli pauses, sees no one here. Then Chambers rustles into view. He approaches her, with:

CIAVELLI
'Scuse me. Is Julie Desmond here?

CHAMBERS
Yes sir. But I'm sorry, infants aren't allowed on the ward.

CIAVELLI
*But this one is **hers**.*

CHAMBERS
It's for the child's own protection, sir . . .

INTERCUT—TOWARD HOSPITAL ROOM

Gannon emerges, shutting the door after him. He looks up with interest as he hears:

> CIAVELLI'S VOICE (O.S.)
> *My name's Ciavelli. Will you tell Julie I'm here . . .?*

ANGLE—FAVORING CIAVELLI

Gannon approaches as:

> CIAVELLI (cont'd)
> *We got a little problem with the baby . . .*

> GANNON
> *I'll take care of it, Chambers . . .*
>   (as Chambers exits)
> *I'm Doctor Gannon, Mr. Ciavelli. Julie's surgeon.*

> CIAVELLI
> *Nice to meetcha, Doctor. It's my Tony—he's ten years old.*

INTERCUT—THE KIDS

The older ones point to the youngest——a 3-year-old.

BACK TO CIAVELLI AND GANNON

> CIAVELLI (cont'd)
> *He looks like he may have the flu. My wife don't think that's so good for little Tina. . .*

> GANNON
> *Your wife is a very wise woman.*

> CIAVELLI
> *Six kids and one on the way. You call that wise??*
>   (shrugs it away)
> *We couldn't find Tom, and Julie's parents weren't home. All we could do was leave a message for 'em. So . . .*

He places the baby in Gannon's arms. Gannon smiles down at the sleeping infant.

GANNON

Well, she looks pretty healthy . . . but we'd better keep her isolated for a while.
(then)
I'll take care of her, Mr. Ciavelli.

CIAVELLI

Thanks, Doctor. Tell Julie we send our love. Okay?

GANNON

Okay.

Ciavelli exits. HOLD ON Gannon, with the baby. She begins to WHIMPER a bit in his arms.

GANNON

Here now, young lady, no complaining . . .

He sees Chambers hurrying by, carrying a basin.

GANNON (cont'd)

Chambers—will you take the baby to Pediatrics? She——

CHAMBERS

Sorry, Doctor. I can't now. I'm in the middle of Mr. Gruber's bath . . .

The PHONE IS RINGING on the Ward Desk, under:

GANNON

I think she needs changing.

Chambers looks around, sees the Orderly wheeling a food cart nearby. She calls to him:

CHAMBERS

George! Get Doctor Gannon some diapers!
(then)
Ooh, that phone . . .!
(answers it)
Four-West, Miss Chambers. . . .
(listens, then)
Yes sir, he's right here.

She hands the phone to Gannon, with:

CHAMBERS (cont'd)
For you. The Mayor's office.

ANGLE—FAVORING GANNON

The baby lets out a loud WAIL, and keeps on WAILING under:

CHAMBERS (cont'd)
Me too, doll. I didn't vote for him either.

She hurries away. Gannon tries to placate the baby as best he can——while speaking into the phone. The baby keeps on WAILING under:

GANNON (into phone)
Doctor Gannon . . .
   (listens, then)
Yes, Mr. Mayor . . .
   (then)
Well, at the moment I have a very sexy young lady in my arms. Yes, that's her. A woman of very definite opinions . . .
   (listens, then)
Well, the telethon starts at 10 p.m. and goes on all night. You can stop in anytime you like.
   (then)
Thanks, Mr. Mayor. See you then.

He hangs up, gives the SQUAWLING baby a rueful look.

GANNON (cont'd)
And I thought I could handle women . . .

CUT TO:
EXT. MEDICAL CENTER—FULL SHOT—NIGHT

A car parks at the curb in F.G. MRS. KELLER——Julie's mother——gets out. She's a chic, fashionable suburban housewife, 40-ish, attractive, genuinely concerned about her daughter. She hurries into the building.

CUT TO:
INT. HOSPITAL ROOM—FAVORING JULIE—NIGHT

in bed, looking weary, trying to find a comfortable position. She has an I.V. in her arm. Mrs. Keller appears at the door, worried.

MRS. KELLER (softly)

Julie . . .?

JULIE (wan smile)

Hi, mother . . .

MRS. KELLER

Good heavens, child, what's happened to you . . .?

JULIE

One of those silly attacks. Doctor Gannon did some excavating, and now I'm fine, mother. Really.

MRS. KELLER

Well what was it?

JULIE

My old friend that's spelled with eighty syllables. But Doctor Gannon has it all fixed now.

MRS. KELLER

Well I'm so relieved. Your father and I have been frantic, Julie. If Mr. Ciavelli hadn't left that message——
(then)
What about Tina? He said he was taking her to the hospital.

JULIE

Just a precaution. One of the Ciavelli kids has the flu.

MRS. KELLER

Well, Tom should have called us. We could have been of some help . . .

JULIE

It all happened so fast . . . and he's been pretty busy . . .

MRS. KELLER (wryly)

Too busy to make a phone call?

JULIE

Mother, Tom knows you and Dad don't exactly approve of him.

ANGLE—TOWARD THE DOOR

Gannon appears in the doorway. He pauses as he hears:

MRS. KELLER'S VOICE (O.S.)
*We don't **disapprove** of Tom either, dear. It's just that his back-*
ground—his attitudes—are so different, so utterly unlike yours . . .

JULIE'S VOICE (O.S.)
Maybe that's why I love him. Because he is different . . .

GANNON'S POV—FAVORING JULIE

JULIE (cont'd)
*He's had a hard time all his life. He **needs** someone to love him,*
to help him, to——to——
Her voice breaks. She turns away, fighting tears.
BACK TO GANNON

He decides it's time to break it up. So:

GANNON (knocks on open door)
May I come in?

Mrs. Keller turns. Julie sniffs away her tears, grateful for the
interruption.

JULIE
Doctor Gannon—this is my mother, Mrs. Keller.

GANNON
Nice to meet you, Mrs. Keller. Lights out now, Julie. You need all
the rest you can get.

JULIE
Is Tina all right?

GANNON (nods)
She's just assumed full command of the Pediatrics Ward.

MRS. KELLER
The baby can stay with us, Julie. Your father and I would love a
chance to spoil her.

JULIE
Mother—I don't know——

GANNON
Sounds like a good idea, Julie. I'm sure she'd be happier with her
grandparents.
   (then)
Now get some sleep, Julie.

MRS. KELLER (kisses her)
Good night, dear. I'll check with you in the morning.

JULIE
'Night, mother.

Gannon turns off the lights. He and Mrs. Keller exit.

INT. WARD CORRIDOR—GANNON, MRS. KELLER—NIGHT

They step out of the room. As Gannon shuts the door:

MRS. KELLER
Doctor Gannon—will Julie really be all right?

GANNON
There's no built-in guarantee, but she's doing very well.

MRS. KELLER
I——imagine all this is rather expensive. I'd like to arrange to take
care of the bills.

GANNON
There aren't any bills, Mrs. Keller. She'll pay what she and Tom
can afford.

MRS. KELLER
*Surely my daughter isn't a **charity** patient. My husband and I **can***
pay her expenses.

GANNON
*In this case, **Julie's** husband is the responsible party. Have you dis-*
cussed it with Tom?

MRS. KELLER
Well, no-oo . . .
   (then)
How well do you know Tom, Doctor?

GANNON (smiles)
I know he's pretty independent, if that's what you mean.

MRS. KELLER (edgily)
*Yes. "Independent". And somewhat impractical. I'm not trying to interfere with my daughter's marriage, Doctor. I'd simply like to **help** them.*

GANNON
That's very nice of you, Mrs. Keller, but I think you should discuss it with them.

A beat. She glares at him, stung by the truth. Then, before she can find the proper reply:

GANNON (cont'd)
Excuse me. I'll see about releasing Tina . . .

He hurries O.S. HOLD ON Mrs. Keller, simmering in frustration.

CUT TO:
EXT. MEDICAL CENTER—A CITY BUS—NIGHT

stops in F.G., at the nearest corner. Tom disembarks. The bus moves O.S. TRUCK WITH Tom toward the building. Suddenly he stops, halted by:

HIS POV—TOWARD THE BUILDING

Mrs. Keller hurries out of the building, carrying the baby. PAN WITH her to the car parked at the curb.

BACK TO TOM

staring——unsure, confused. Then, realizing:

TOM
Hey——!

TRUCK WITH him as he runs toward the car.

ANGLE—AT THE CAR

Mrs. Keller sets the baby down on the front seat, swaddled in blankets. She starts the car, drives away. PAN AWAY TO Tom, approaching at a dead run. He races into F.G., stares after the vanishing car. A moment of confused exasperation, then he races into the Medical Center.

CUT TO:
INT. WARD CORRIDOR—THE ORDERLY—NIGHT

sweeping the floor near the elevators. The doors open. Tom charges out, almost knocks the Orderly over.

> ORDERLY
> *Hey—watch it, man. . .!*

Tom hurries toward Julie's room, but:

> ORDERLY (cont'd)
> *Your wife's asleep, Tom. Better not wake her up.*

> TOM (a beat, unsure)
> *Where's Gannon?*

> ORDERLY
> *Try the Theatre Arts Building. They're getting ready for the telethon.*

As Tom hurries away:

CUT TO:
INT. SOUND STAGE—FULL SHOT—NIGHT

The "arena" area is cluttered with TV cameras, cables, assorted equipment. CREWMEN are at work, setting up. At one side, there's a lo-ong bank of tables with telephones. PAN SLOWLY to this area, and ZOOM IN ON Lochner and Gannon, discussing it. Various placards decorate the B.G., heralding the "*NEW COMMUNITY CLINIC*".

> GANNON
> *And as the donations are phoned in, the computer records them, and the totals are flashed on that chart.*

> LOCHNER
> *The Mayor called awhile ago. He'll definitely make an appearance.*

TOM

Doctor Gannon——!

Gannon turns, sees Tom storming toward him.

GANNON

Excuse me, Paul . . .

ANGLE—FAVORING TOM

As Gannon joins him:

TOM (furious)
*My mother-in-law just drove away with Tina. What's my kid doing
with her??*

Gannon steers him to a secluded area, as:

GANNON
*Tina couldn't stay with the Ciavellis. One of their kids has the flu
. . .*

TOM
*She can stay with **me**, can't she!*

GANNON (evenly)
*Tom, the baby's much better off with her grandparents. You'll be
working every day, and——*

TOM (heatedly)
*I'm **not** working! I just lost the job——my boat——everything!*

GANNON (sincerely)
I'm sorry. I didn't know.

TOM
*Great, huh? My boat's repossessed, and I can't earn a living without
it. All I need is **one** payment to get it out of hock . . . a lousy hundred
and thirty-five dollars.*

GANNON
Look, if I can help in any way——

TOM (bitterly)
*How—build me a clinic? You fat cats and your lousy charity! You
want people to be hungry so you can feel noble—so you can build
clinics and do telethons!*

(building in anger)
When a man's hungry, he wants a sandwich—but **you** *have to build him the whole restaurant!*
(then)
I don't need a telethon to raise what I need, Doc. I'll get it my **own** *way.*

He starts away. Gannon grabs his arm, with:

GANNON
Wait a minute, Tom——

TOM (defiantly)
You heard me, Doc: my **own** *way.*

He pulls away and strides out. HOLD ON Gannon, gazing after him.

FADE OUT.

END ACT THREE

ACT FOUR

FADE IN:

EXT. WATERFRONT BAR—TO ESTABLISH—NIGHT

The neon sign flashes *"THE SAND BAR"*.

INT. WATERFRONT BAR—FAVORING TOM—NIGHT

A sleazy tavern; marine decor; three or four patrons in various phases of inebriation. Tom, seated at the bar, is entering the final phase. He drains his glass, signals the BARTENDER.

TOM

Another one, Frank.

BARTENDER

No more, Tom.

TOM (indignant)
Whattaya mean, no more? My credit's good!

BARTENDER

*Not **that** good.*

As Tom starts to leave in a huff, an over-aged hooker named GLORIA sidles up to Tom, with:

GLORIA

Hi. You like wrestling?

TOM

What . . .?

GLORIA

Frank, put on the wrestling.

She gestures to the TV. The bartender climbs on a stepstool to turn on the TV set.

ANGLE—FAVORING BARTENDER

working the TV set, flipping the channels. Gloria drapes herself over Tom, with:

> GLORIA
> *It's a fake, but I dig it. We got too much reality anyway. Reality's a big drag——*

> TOM (suddenly)
> *Hey, Frank—let's see that!*

ZOOM IN CLOSER ON the TV set. Gannon is addressing the camera——seen but not heard.

> TOM (cont'd)
> *Turn it up!*

The bartender turns up the sound, and we hear:

> GANNON
> *—again, the number is 626-0799——the mail contributions, the telephone pledges, the personal donation-boxes located throughout the city—have been extremely encouraging. But we need more, a lot more. With your help, we can make this Clinic the finest in the world—offering the best medical talent and facilities to anyone in the community who requires medical care. There'll be no fees, no charges, no cost to anyone after the Clinic opens. But right now, the cost is high——*

> GLORIA
> *Is **that** what those money-boxes are for? They're all over the waterfront. How much do they hold anyway?*

> BARTENDER
> *I dunno. Maybe fifty, sixty dollars . . .*

Tom turns, stares O.S., toward the door. The bartender flips the channel to the wrestling matches.

> GLORIA
> *Now that's more like it.*
> (to Tom)
> *Hey, where you going?*

ANGLE—FAVORING TOM

TRUCK WITH him to the donation-box display near the door. It's mounted like a gumball machine. He shakes it. The coins rattle noisily. It's about three-quarters filled.

> TOM
> *Fifty, sixty bucks in **this** . . .?*

> BARTENDER
> *Sure. Maybe more, even.*

Tom eyes the display thoughtfully. Then he walks, a bit unsteadily to the phone booth. TRUCK WITH him. He fumbles for a dime, deposits, dials the number. The booth door remains open as he speaks into the phone:

> TOM (thickly)
> *H'lo Telethon? I wanna talk to Gannon. Doctor Jo-seph Gan-non.*

INT. SOUND STAGE—OPERATOR #1 AT TELETHON— INTERCUTTING—NIGHT

> OPERATOR #1
> *He's on another line right now. Any message, sir.*

> TOM
> *Yeah, I got a message for him. Tell him I think his clinic stinks. Tell him it's nothing but a crummy monument to his crummy ego. It—*
>   (CLICK, at the other end of the line)
> *H'lo? **Hello??***

ANGEL—TOM'S POV

The donation-box display. The IMAGE BLURS, then SNAPS INTO FOCUS AGAIN. ZOOM IN CLOSE ON the display, showing the coins.

BACK TO TOM

standing near the booth, staring at the donation-box. He considers it carefully. Then he turns back to the booth.

ANGLE—AT THE BOOTH

Tom fishes out another coin, deposits it, dials a number.

> TOM (into phone)
> *H'lo? Is Gannon still busy? I wanna talk to him.*

INT. SOUND STAGE—TELETHON—WITH OPERATOR #2—INTERCUTTING—NIGHT

> OPERATOR #2
> *He's busy, sir—Do you wish to make a contribution?*

> TOM
> *No, I'm not making any contributions to your stinking clinic! How much money you got so far?*

> OPERATOR #2
> *I don't have that figure, but if you wish to add to—*

> TOM
> *Well, instead of **adding** money, you can start **subtracting**. You're gonna start **losing** money any minute now!*

He hangs up, lurches out of the booth. Nobody at the bar is paying any attention to him. He looks around, sees a belaying pin on the wall——part of the marine decor. He yanks it off the wall, hefts it thoughtfully, then heads for the door. TRUCK WITH him. He stops at the donation-box display, hefts the belaying pin like a club, takes careful aim.

CLOSE ANGLE—UP AT TOM

He lifts the belaying pin——brings it down, hard.

CLOSE ANGLE—THE DONATION-BOX DISPLAY

The pin SHATTERS the plastic container. Coins spurt and jingle in all directions.

INTERCUT—AT THE BAR

Bartender, Gloria, others——they turn around, startled.

> BARTENDER
> *Hey–what're you doing??*

ANGLE—FAVORING TOM

Using his jacket as a sack, he gathers the coins in it. Holding the belaying pin in one hand, his jacket full of coins in the other, he rushes out.

> BARTENDER
> *He's flipped out . . .*

> GLORIA
> *Call the cops . . .*

CUT TO:
EXT. WATERFRONT STREET—TOM—NIGHT

TRUCK WITH him——running, running. Now he stops, as he approaches a small, greasy-spoon cafe. He looks through the glass door, into the lighted interior.

HIS POV—INTO THE CAFE

A donation-box display is on the counter, near the cash register. The CASHIER (female) is at the open register, counting out the day's receipts. She takes the cash drawer and walks in the back.

He looks around quickly, hurries into the cafe.

INT. CAFE—NIGHT

as Tom approaches the counter.

CLOSE ANGLE—THE DONATION-BOX DISPLAY

The belaying pin comes down hard, SHATTERS the plastic con-

tainer. He scoops up the bills and some coins and runs out as
the cashier runs in, startled. She runs to phone, picks it up, as
we:

CUT TO:
INT. SOUND STAGE—FAVORING
TELETHON CHART—NIGHT

A pretty girl takes down the old total, replaces it with the new
one, as we hear:

> ANNOUNCER'S VOICE (O.S.)
> *And the telethon's grand total now stands at $887,650!!*

INT. CLEANING SHOP—THROUGH
GLASS DOOR—NIGHT

The shop is closed, dark. Tom can be seen on the street, rushing
up to the glass door. He SMASHES it with the belaying pin. PULL
BACK as he steps through the shattered door, to the donation-box
display located just inside the shop. Again he lifts the belaying
pin——swings——and SHATTERS the plastic container. Coins
explode in all directions.

INT. SOUND STAGE—THE
TELETHON CHART—NIGHT

The girl places a new total over the old one as:

> ANNOUNCER'S VOICE (O.S.)
> *And our latest telephone pledges bring our total to $891,855!!*

INTERCUT—CLOSE—TOM

SMASHING another donation-box.

INT. SOUND STAGE—THE
TELETHON CHART—NIGHT

Another new total is placed on the chart, as:

> ANNOUNCER'S VOICE (O.S.)
> *...an even $902,000! Keep those calls coming in, friends! Remember, our goal is—*

INTERCUT—CLOSE—TOM

SMASHES another donation-box.

INT. SOUND STAGE—FAVORING GANNON—NIGHT

seated at the Celebrity Table, speaking into a phone. Other phones are being handled by entertainers, civic leaders, etc. A SINGER OR MUSICIAN is performing for the TV cameras in B.G. Lochner approaches Gannon, as:

> GANNON (into phone)
> *Yes ma'am, we'll be happy to mention your name on the air. Thanks again for your pledge.*

He hangs up, makes a note on a pad beside the phone.

> LOCHNER (upset)
> *Joe . . .*
>   (Gannon looks up)
> *The police just called. Somebody's been breaking into the donation boxes.*

PUSH IN ON Gannon, looking off, grim.

EXT. HARBOR AREA—INTO PHONE BOOTH—NIGHT

Tom, still drunk, his pockets bulging with coins, is speaking into the phone. He still carries the belaying pin.

> TOM (into phone)
> *Tom Desmond. You heard me, Charlie—**Tom Desmond.***

INT. CHARLIE'S ROOM—CLOSE—CHARLIE—NIGHT

in bed, rumpled, indignant. From O.S., the SOUNDS of the water-front can be HEARD. As he speaks into the phone, INTERCUT AS NEEDED TO TOM IN PHONE BOOTH.

> CHARLIE
> *You crazy, Tom? It's the middle of the night. Whattaya want?*

> TOM
> *My boat. I've got the money I owe you, Charlie. Now I want my boat——*

> CHARLIE
> *You **are** crazy, kid. The messenger came with the money a few hours ago. The boat's back in the slip.*

> TOM
> *What messenger? I didn't send any money!*

> CHARLIE
> *Well, somebody did. Now, knock off the jokes, okay? I'm tired.*

Charlie hangs up, goes back to sleep.

EXT. HARBOR AREA—INTO PHONE
BOOTH—NIGHT

> TOM (into phone)
> *Charlie? Hello——??*

But Charlie has hung up. Bewildered, Tom hangs up——frowning. He steps out of the booth, looks around, hurries toward the slips.

EXT. WATERFRONT STREET—A
POLICE CAR—NIGHT

speeds THROUGH THE FRAME, SIREN SCREAMING.

EXT. HARBOR AREA—AT TOM'S SLIP—NIGHT

Tom runs TOWARD CAMERA. As he reaches F.G., he slows to a stop, stares PAST CAMERA, at:

HIS POV—HIS BOAT

sits in the slip.

BACK TO TOM

disbelief, confusion. Then, slowly, the incredulity fades——and the sense of futility engulfs him, the futility of his anger, defiance, wasted emotion.

CLOSE ANGLE—INTO THE WATER

The belaying pin SPLASHES into the water, floats away. ANGLE UP TO Tom, on the edge of the slip——staring into the water. Beaten, exhausted by the futile waste of energy and emotion, he sags to a sitting position on a coil of line. He's alone on the deserted slip, his face in his hands, the picture of abject despair. From O.S., we HEAR the distant SOUND of the approaching POLICE SIREN. Tom hears it too, but he doesn't move.

CUT TO:
INT. HOSPITAL ROOM—CLOSE—JULIE—DAY

sitting up in bed. Her eyes are red from recent tears. She has regained her composure, but the shock——the disappointment——the feeling of betrayal——have left their marks. Her voice is low, controlled, with only a rough edge of emotion.

> JULIE
> *What will they do to him, Doctor Gannon . . .?*

PULL BACK to include Gannon at her bedside, as:

> GANNON
> *With Tom's record, I'm afraid the courts may not be lenient.*

> JULIE
> *Taking that money was so foolish–so unnecessary . . .*

> GANNON
> *And money that could have done so much good. Like a respirator that could save someone who's fighting for breath.*
> (pause)
> *Julie, what made him do it?*

> JULIE (softly)
> *I'm not sure. But I do know that Tom felt no matter how long he lived, he'd never be able to wash off the grime from the ghettos where he was raised.*

GANNON

But he took money from the very people whom we intend to help.

JULIE

*Maybe that's the key, Doctor—I mean Tom's hating the offer of an outstretched hand. He was **raised** on welfare checks. But they weren't enough to support his family. His father had to sneak out and find a job. When he was caught working—working!—he lost his welfare **and** his job. His last shred of dignity was taken away from him. Tom never forgot that. Never . . .*
    (then wearily)
I tried to make him see things differently, but—
    (helpless shrug)

ANGLE—FAVORING GANNON

GANNON

I'm sure you did, Julie—
    (a beat, then, rising)
The police called a while ago. Tom has asked to see me. Anything you'd like me to tell him?

JULIE (a beat)

Just tell him I'm sorry.

Gannon presses her hand, and exits. HOLD ON Julie, staring at her thoughts. One tear trickles down her cheek. Just one.

CUT TO:
INT. JAIL CELL—THROUGH THE BARS—DAY

Gannon approaches, preceded by an OFFICER. The officer unlocks the cell coor, opens it. Gannon enters the cell, looking PAST CAMERA. The door CLANGS shut behind him.

GANNON

Tom . . .

HIS POV—TOM

stands at the cell window, his BACK TO Gannon and CAMERA. His posture indicates his feeling of defeat, humiliation.

> TOM
>
> *Y'know, Juvie Hall had a better view.*

ANGLE—FAVORING GANNON

He doesn't reply. He waits. Finally Tom turns to face him. He needs a shave; his eyes are sunken, hollow. He wears his guilt like a leper wears a bell.

> TOM (cont'd)
>
> *Doesn't matter though. I've got nothing to look for.*

> GANNON
>
> *You wanted to see me?*

> TOM
>
> *Believe it or not, I——I——wanted to thank you. For getting my boat out of hock. You're the guy who did it, aren't you?*
>   (Gannon nods)
> *I'll pay you back. Every cent. It may take a while, though . . .*
>   (sudden thought)
> *In fact, Julie can sell the boat and keep the money and——*
>   (stops; futility again)
> *How is she? Is she all right . . .?*

> GANNON
>
> *She's fine. She'll be out of bed by next week.*

ANGLE—FAVORING TOM

He nods——lost, helpless. SITS DOWN ON THE BUNK. Then——

> TOM
>
> *Boy, talk about a dummy—Here I had everything going for me—a wife who almost killed herself trying to help me, a healthy baby, friends who gave me every break in the book. And I blew it.*

ANGLE—FAVORING GANNON

> GANNON
>
> *I'd say you built up a lot of scar tissue when you were a kid. You*

decided that charity was a plot against your pride and dignity . . .
kindness was something that blew up in your face . . .

                              TOM
In some cases I was right.

                            GANNON
*In **some** cases. But Tom, you may have to look for it, there **is** kindness*
in this world. Kindness and decency. And people in the world who'd
*rather love than hate. When you start accepting **them**, maybe they'll*
*accept **you**.*

He turns, raps on the bars.

                      GANNON (cont'd)
Guard!

The officer appears, unlocks and opens the cell door. Gannon
steps out. The door CLANGS shut. As he starts away, Tom steps
to the bars with:

                              TOM
Doctor Gannon . . .

Gannon turns.

CLOSE SHOT—TOM

Speaks to Gannon through the bars of the cell door:

                         TOM (cont'd)
Tell Julie—tell her I'm grateful. She tried to love me . . . a guy
can't ask any more than that.

ANGLE—FAVORING GANNON

                  GANNON (a beat; impressed)
Good luck, Tom.

Gannon walks away, HOLD ON Tom, watching him go. Then
Tom turns away, walks to the cell window, and stands in the patch
of sunlight——looking out.

                                        FADE OUT.

                         THE END

A teleplay by Don Brinkley upon which a MEDICAL CENTER television series
episode entitled "Countdown" was produced © Metro-Goldwyn-Mayer Inc.
MCMLXX.

ANTISOCIAL BEHAVIOR, NO PUNISHMENT

In a second version of the story, Tom is chased by the police, but he eventually escapes to Mexico. The relevant portions of the altered script follow:

ACT FOUR[1]

FADE IN:

EXT. WATERFRONT BAR—TO ESTABLISH—NIGHT

The neon sign flashes *"THE SAND BAR"*.

INT. WATERFRONT BAR—FAVORING TOM—NIGHT

A sleazy tavern; marine decor; three or four patrons in various phases of inebriation. Tom, seated at the bar, is entering the final phase. He drains his glass, signals the BARTENDER.

TOM
Another one, Frank.

BARTENDER
No more, Tom.

TOM (indignant)
Whattaya mean, no more? My credit's good!

BARTENDER
*Not **that** good.*

As Tom starts to leave in a huff, an over-aged hooker named GLORIA sidles up to Tom, with:

GLORIA
Hi. You like wrestling?

TOM
What . . .?

GLORIA
Frank, put on the wrestling.

She gestures to the TV. The bartender climbs on a stepstool to turn on the TV set.

[1]A portion of a teleplay by Don Brinkley upon which a MEDICAL CENTER television series episode entitled "Countdown" was produced © Metro-Goldwyn-Mayer Inc. MCMLXX.

ANGLE—FAVORING BARTENDER

working the TV set, flipping the channels. Gloria drapes herself over Tom, with:

> GLORIA
>
> *It's a fake, but I dig it. We got too much reality anyway. Reality's a big drag——*

> TOM (suddenly)
>
> *Hey, Frank—let's see that!*

ZOOM IN CLOSER ON the TV set. Gannon is addressing the camera——seen but not heard.

> TOM (cont'd)
>
> *Turn it up!*

The bartender turns up the sound, and we hear:

> GANNON
>
> *—again, the number is 626-0799——the mail contributions, the telephone pledges, the personal donation-boxes located throughout the city—have been extremely encouraging. But we need more, a lot more. With your help, we can make this Clinic the finest in the world—offering the best medical talent and facilities to anyone in the community who requires medical care. There'll be no fees, no charges, no cost to anyone after the Clinic opens. But right now, the cost is high——*

> GLORIA
>
> *Is **that** what those money-boxes are for? They're all over the waterfront. How much do they hold anyway?*
>
> BARTENDER
>
> *I dunno. Maybe fifty, sixty dollars . . .*

Tom turns, stares O.S., toward the door. The bartender flips the channel to the wrestling matches.

GLORIA

Now that's more like it.
  (to Tom)
Hey, where you going?

ANGLE—FAVORING TOM

TRUCK WITH him to the donation-box display near the door. It's mounted like a gumball machine. He shakes it. The coins rattle noisily. It's about three-quarters filled.

TOM

*Fifty, sixty bucks in **this** . . .?*

BARTENDER

Sure. Maybe more, even.

Tom eyes the display thoughtfully. Then he walks, a bit unsteadily to the phone booth. TRUCK WITH him. He fumbles for a dime, deposits, dials the number. The booth door remains open as he speaks into the phone:

TOM (thickly)

H'lo Telethon? I wanna talk to Gannon. Doctor Jo-seph Gan-non.

INT. SOUND STAGE—OPERATOR #1 AT TELETHON—INTERCUTTING—NIGHT

OPERATOR #1

He's on another line right now. Any message, sir.

TOM

Yeah, I got a message for him. Tell him I think his clinic stinks. Tell him it's nothing but a crummy monument to his crummy ego. It——
  (CLICK, at the other end of the line)
*H'lo? **Hello??***

ANGLE—TOM'S POV

The donation-box display. The IMAGE BLURS, then SNAPS INTO FOCUS AGAIN. ZOOM IN CLOSE ON the display, showing the coins.

BACK TO TOM

standing near the booth, staring at the donation-box. He considers it carefully. Then he turns back to the booth.

ANGLE—AT THE BOOTH

Tom fishes out another coin, deposits it, dials a number.

> TOM (into phone)
> *H'lo? Is Gannon still busy? I wanna talk to him.*

INT. SOUND STAGE—TELETHON—WITH OPERATOR #2—INTERCUTTING—NIGHT

> OPERATOR #2
> *He's busy, sir—Do you wish to make a contribution?*

> TOM
> *No, I'm not making any contributions to your stinking clinic! How much money you got so far?*

> OPERATOR #2
> *I don't have that figure, but if you wish to add to—*

> TOM
> *Well, instead of **adding** money, you can start **subtracting**. You're gonna start **losing** money any minute now!*

He hangs up, lurches out of the booth. Nobody at the bar is paying any attention to him. He looks around, sees a belaying pin on the wall——part of the marine decor. He yanks it off the wall, hefts it thoughtfully, then heads for the door. TRUCK WITH him. He stops at the donation-box display, hefts the belaying pin like a club, takes careful aim.

CLOSE ANGLE—UP AT TOM

He lifts the belaying pin——brings it down, hard.

CLOSE ANGLE—THE DONATION-BOX DISPLAY

The pin SHATTERS the plastic container. Coins spurt and jingle in all directions.

INTERCUT—AT THE BAR

Bartender, Gloria, others——they turn around, startled.

> BARTENDER
> *Hey, what're you doing??*

ANGLE—FAVORING TOM

Using his jacket as a sack, he gathers the coins in it. Holding the belaying pin in one hand, his jacket full of coins in the other, he rushes out.

> BARTENDER
> *He's flipped out . . .*

> GLORIA
> *Call the cops . . .*

CUT TO:
EXT. WATERFRONT STREET—TOM—NIGHT

TRUCK WITH him——running, running. Now he stops, as he approaches a small, greasy-spoon cafe. He looks through the glass door, into the lighted interior.

HIS POV—INTO THE CAFE

A donation-box display is on the counter, near the cash register. The CASHIER (female) is at the open register, counting out the day's receipts. She takes the cash drawer and walks in the back.

He looks around quickly, hurries into the cafe.

INT. CAFE—NIGHT

as Tom approaches the counter.

CLOSE ANGLE—THE DONATION-BOX DISPLAY

The belaying pin comes down hard, SHATTERS the plastic container. He scoops up the bills and some coins and runs out as the cashier runs in, startled. She runs to phone, picks it up, as we:

CUT TO:
INT. SOUND STAGE—FAVORING TELETHON CHART—NIGHT

A pretty girl takes down the old total, replaces it with the new one, as we hear:

>   ANNOUNCER'S VOICE (O.S.)
>   *And the telethon's grand total now stands at $887,650!!*

INT. CLEANING SHOP—THROUGH
GLASS DOOR—NIGHT

The shop is closed, dark. Tom can be seen on the street, rushing up to the glass door. He SMASHES it with the belaying pin. PULL BACK as he steps through the shattered door, to the donation-box display located just inside the shop. Again he lifts the belaying pin——swings——and SHATTERS the plastic container. Coins explode in all directions.

INT. SOUND STAGE—THE TELETHON
CHART—NIGHT

The girl places a new total over the old one as:

>   ANNOUNCER'S VOICE (O.S.)
>   *And our latest telephone pledges bring our total to $891,855!!*

INTERCUT—CLOSE—TOM

SMASHING another donation-box.

INT. SOUND STAGE—THE
TELETHON CHART—NIGHT

Another new total is placed on the chart, as:

> ANNOUNCER'S VOICE (O.S.)
> . . . *an even $902,000! It's almost dawn friends—let's see if we
> can reach a million by sunrise!*

INTERCUT—CLOSE—TOM—DAY

Dawn is just breaking. He SMASHES another donation-box, scoops
up the bills and some of the change and hurries around the corner.

ANGLE AROUND CORNER—DAY

Tom hurries around intent on making a run for it, stops quickly
as he sees a police car drive up at the end of the street and stop.
Tom ducks down into the shadows of a basement approach to
an empty building. He waits there as one of the policemen gets
out of the car, sees nothing——then gets back in and the car cruises
past where he is hiding.

When the police car is out of sight, Tom comes up to the walk
and hurries out in the opposite direction taken by the police car.

EXT. WATERFRONT STREET—TRUCKING
SHOT—DAY

It's just about dawn. The half-light of the sunrise underscores the
melancholy atmosphere of the gray, deserted street. Tom is
running, running——the jacket full of coins slung over his shoul-
der, the belaying pin still in his hand. Now he HEARS the
SOUND, O.S., of an approaching POLICE SIREN. He turns to
look.

HIS POV—A POLICE CAR

SIREN SCREAMING, red light spinning, the squad car careens around a corner, speeds TOWARD CAMERA.

BACK TO TOM

Panic. He looks around for an escape, vanishes down an alley, An instant later, the police car speeds into view, brakes to a SCREECHING STOP, backs up, and heads down the alley in pursuit; he

EXT. HARBOR AREA—TOM—DAY

races out from between buildings, finds himself near the piers. The POLICE SIREN approaches O.S. He vaults over a stack of kegs and crates, heads toward the piers, O.S. A beat, then the police car appears, fishtails to a stop, SIREN GROWLING to silence. TWO OFFICERS get out. They can go no farther by car; they pursue on foot.

ANGLE—TOM

running TOWARD CAMERA. As he races, breathless, wild-eyed, into F.G., another APPROACHING SIREN is HEARD O.S. He stops——stares PAST CAMERA.

TOM'S POV—ANOTHER POLICE CAR

speeds TOWARD CAMERA, toward Tom. It goes as far as it can, SCREECHES to a stop. TWO MORE OFFICERS hop out.

BACK TO TOM

trapped——ahead of him and behind him. Desperate now, he races out on a pier. There's no place else to go.

INTERCUT—POLICE OFFICERS

in pursuit, on foot——still a distance behind him.

TRUCKING SHOT—TOM

running madly along the pier. He's still holding the belaying pin in one hand, the jacket full of coins in the other. Now, inexorably, he is at the end of the pier. Dead end. He turns for another look at his pursuers.

TOM'S POV—THE OFFICERS

One of the officers is a few paces ahead of the others, still a good 20 to 30 yeards away from Tom. He draws his gun, and shouts:

OFFICER

Hold it, Desmond——

BACK TO TOM

A BOAT'S CLAXON is HEARD O.S., but he doesn't notice. In a gesture of last-ditch defiance, he hurls the belaying pin at the on-coming officers——turns——and dives off the end of the pier.

INTERCUT—THE OFFICERS

They reach the end of the pier, look off——into the water. The BOAT'S CLAXON is HEARD AGAIN, O.S.

INTERCUT—A SMALL TUGBOAT

in the channel, heading directly for the spot where Tom hit the water.

ANGLE—INTO WATER

Tom surfaces, still clutching the heavy jacket full of money. He starts to swim, when he HEARS the SOUND of the BOAT'S CLAXON, O.S., directly upon him. ZOOM IN CLOSE ON Tom for his reaction: sheer, helpless panic.

TOM'S POV—UP AT TUGBOAT

CHUGGING directly AT CAMERA——until it FILLS THE FRAME COMPLETELY.

CUT TO:
INT. HOSPITAL ROOM—CLOSE—JULIE—DAY

lying in bed, staring at the ceiling. Motionless, uncaring. Her eyes
are red, her face tear-streaked. A tray of food is on the bedside
table, untouched. PULL BACK to include Gannon, entering the
room. He looks at the tray, looks down at Julie.

> GANNON (firmly)
> *Four days, Julie. How long do you expect to go on without food?*
>   (no response)
> *Look, young lady: Tom's gone. They've run out of places to look
> for him. It's a sad, miserable, unpleasant situation—but you'll have
> to accept it.*

> JULIE
> *No. He's alive. I know he is.*

> GANNON
> *Do you think starving yourself to death can bring him back?*
>   (she turns away)
> *All right. We'll have to feed you intravenously.*

> JULIE (flatly)
> *Don't bother, Doctor.*

> GANNON
> *Sorry. It's my job to keep you alive.*

> JULIE (wearily)
> *What for?*

> GANNON
> *Well, for one thing, you've got a 3-month-old baby. Or have you
> forgotten about her?*

Zingo, Touché. She stiffens ever so slightly and turns to look at
him. Gannon pursues his advantage:

> GANNON (cont'd)
> *If you want to punish yourself for Tom's mistakes, that's your affair.
> But why punish Tina?*

> JULIE
> *I'm not punishing anyone . . .*

> GANNON
> *Aren't you? Tina's father ran out on her. Now her mother's doing the very same thing!*
>   (adjusts bedside table)
> *Now, stop acting like a martyr and eat your lunch.*

A beat. Then, reluctantly, Julie forces herself to sit up in bed. Gannon adjusts the tray on the table. As he does so, Nurse Chambers enters with:

> CHAMBERS
> *Letter for you, Julie. From Mexico.*

> JULIE (puzzled)
> *Mexico . . .?*

Chambers hands her the letter, and exits.

ANGLE—FAVORING JULIE

She stares at the letter with increasing disbelief.

> JULIE (hushed; unsure)
> *It's——from Tom . . .*
>   (then, the revelation; eager; excited)
> *He's alive! Doctor Gannon—Tom's **alive!!***

Fumbling eagerly, she struggles to open the envelope. It slips from her fingers. Gannon picks it up, opens it, hands it to her. She unfolds the letter, holds it in trembling hands. DOLLY IN CLOSE as she reads——and we hear:

> TOM'S VOICE (O.S.)
> *"Dear Julie. Just a word to let you know I'm alive and healthy—and a little richer than ever before. As soon as I find a place to live, I'll send the plane-fare for you and Tina. If you don't want to join me, I'll understand. I love you, Julie. I really do . . ."*

Julie looks up——misty-eyed, radiant. She hands the letter to Gannon, with:

> JULIE (eagerly)
> *He's left the country. Wants me to join him as soon as he gets settled.*

PULL BACK to include Gannon, scanning the letter. As:

JULIE (cont'd)
How soon can I go, Doctor? When can I leave here?

GANNON
A few more days . . .
  (then)
Are you sure that's what you want to do?

JULIE
*Of course it is. He's my **husband**! I belong with him!*

ANGLE—FAVORING GANNON

GANNON
You may get hurt again, Julie. Remember—he's a fugitive, he's wanted by the police.

JULIE
Tom's no criminal . . . he's just confused, mixed up. Tina and I can help him. I know we can.

GANNON
He doesn't accept help very graciously. He thinks of it as charity.

JULIE
*You don't understand him, Doctor! You don't know **why** he feels that way.*

GANNON
Do you?

ANGLE—FAVORING JULIE

JULIE
*Yes. He was raised on charity. Welfare checks. They weren't enough to support the family, so his father had to sneak out and find a job. When he was caught working—working, mind you!—he lost his welfare **and** his job. His last shred of dignity. Tom never forgot that. Never . . .*

GANNON
He's been carrying that load around for years. Do you think you can change him?

JULIE

*Well, I know it won't be easy. But I **do** know I have to try. The
simple fact that I love him—that I **want** to be with—may be enough.*

GANNON

*Don't romanticize it, Julie. You'll need a lot more than love. You'll
need strength—wisdom—courage—patience——*

JULIE

And Tom. Most of all, I need Tom. And he needs me.
  (smiles)
*You're not going to talk me out of it, Doctor. I **am** going to Mexico.*

ANGLE—FAVORING GANNON

He studies her for a long moment. She's become eager, animated,
active——a very alive young woman.

GANNON

*Y'know, it's hard to believe you're the same girl I saw a few minutes
ago . . .*

JULIE

I'm not. And frankly, I like me much better now.

GANNON (surrendering)

*Well, if you can do for Tom what he's done for you, we may be
in for a fresh supply of miracles. I wish you luck, Julie . . .*

And surprisingly, he picks up her food tray and starts out.

JULIE

Hey—my lunch . . .!

GANNON

It's cold. I'll get you another one.

He exits. HOLD ON Julie. She picks up Toms' letter, snuggles
down comfortably in bed to read it——savoring it——warm, happy,
anticipating a whole new life.

INT. WARD CORRIDOR—FAVORING GANNON—DAY

TRUCK WITH him to the Ward Desk, where Chambers is working.
He places the tray on the desk, with:

GANNON

Chambers . . .
     (she looks up)
A warm lunch for Julie. And have 'em toss in some enchiladas. She might as well get used to 'em.

Chambers stares after him. He heads down the corridor.

FADE OUT.

THE END

A portion of a teleplay by Don Brinkley upon which a MEDICAL CENTER television series episode entitled "Countdown" was produced © Metro-Goldwyn-Mayer Inc. MCMLXX.

PROSOCIAL BEHAVIOR

In the prosocial version of the story, Tom never breaks into the charity displays, although he seriously considers it, nor does he make any abusive phone calls. The relevant portions of the altered script follow:

ACT FOUR

FADE IN:

EXT. WATERFRONT BAR—TO ESTABLISH—NIGHT

The neon sign flashes *"THE SAND BAR"*.

INT. WATERFRONT BAR—FAVORING TOM—NIGHT

A sleazy tavern; marine decor; three or four patrons in various phases of inebriation. Tom, seated at the bar, is entering the final phase. He drains his glass, signals the BARTENDER.

TOM

Another one, Frank.

BARTENDER

No more, Tom.

TOM (indignant)

Whattaya mean, no more? My credit's good!

BARTENDER

*Not **that** good.*

As Tom starts to leave in a huff, an over-aged hooker named GLORIA sidles up to Tom with:

GLORIA

Hi . . . You like wrestling?

TOM

What . . .?

GLORIA

Frank, put on the wrestling.

She gestures to the TV. The bartender climbs on a stepstool to turn on the TV set.

[1]A portion of a teleplay by Don Brinkley upon which a MEDICAL CENTER television series episode entitled "Countdown" was produced © Metro-Goldwyn-Mayer Inc. MCMLXX.

ANGLE—FAVORING BARTENDER

working the TV set, flipping the channels. Gloria drapes herself over Tom, with:

> GLORIA
> *It's a fake, but I dig it. We got too much reality anyway. Reality's a big drag——*

> TOM (cont'd)
> *Turn it up!*

The bartender turns up the sound, and we hear:

> GANNON
> *—again, the number is 626-0799—the mail contributions, the telephone pledges, the personal donation-boxes located throughout the city—have been extremely encouraging. But we need more, a lot more. With your help, we can make this Clinic the finest in the world—offering the best medical talent and facilities to anyone in the community who requires medical care. There'll be no fees, no charges, no cost to anyone after the Clinic opens. But right now, the cost is high——*

> GLORIA
> *Is **that** what those money-boxes are for? They're all over the waterfront. How much do they hold anyway?*
>
> BARTENDER
> *I dunno. Maybe fifty, sixty dollars . . .*

Tom turns, stares O.S., toward the door. The bartender flips the channel to the wrestling matches.

> GLORIA
> *Now that's more like it.*
> (to Tom)
> *Hey, where you going?*

ANGLE—FAVORING TOM

TRUCK WITH him, walking unsteadily, to the donation-box display near the door. It's mounted like a gumball machine. He shakes it. The coins rattle noisily. It's about three-quarters filled.

> TOM
> *Fifty, sixty bucks in **this**?*

> BARTENDER
> *Sure. Maybe more, even.*

> TOM (thoughtfully)
> *A few of these, and a guy could build his own clinic.*

> BARTENDER
> *Hands off, Tom. That money's for people who need it.*

> TOM (grim)
> *Yeah, right. "People who need it."*

With another look at the donation-box, he lurches out the door.

INT. SOUND STAGE—FAVORING
TELETHON CHART—NIGHT

A pretty girl takes down the old total, replaces it with the new one as we hear:

> ANNOUNCER'S VOICE (O.S.)
> *And the telethon's grand total now stands at $887,650!*

EXT. WATERFRONT STREET—TOM—NIGHT

TRUCK WITH him, walking unsteadily, along the deserted street. Approaching a small, greasy-spoon cafe, he stumbles to a stop and looks through the glass door, into the lighted interior.

HIS POV—INTO THE CAFE

A donation-box display is on the counter, near the cash register. The CASHIER (female) has her back to the door, reading a magazine. ZOOM IN CLOSE ON the donation-box display. The IMAGE BLURS, then SNAPS INTO FOCUS AGAIN.

BACK TO TOM

A long look, then he starts down the street, muttering:

                                        TOM
   Yeah. People who need it.

INT. SOUND STAGE—THE
TELETHON CHART—NIGHT

The girl places a new total over the old one, as:

                        ANNOUNCER'S VOICE (O.S.)
  And our latest telephone pledges bring our total to $891,855!

INT. CLEANING SHOP—THROUGH
GLASS DOOR—NIGHT

The shop is closed, dark. Tom can be seen approaching on the street, through the glass door. Walking unsteadily, he's about to pass the shop—when something attracts him. He stops, walks unsteadily to the glass door, looks inside.

REVERSE ANGLE—TOM'S POV

A donation-box display can be seen just inside the door.

ANGLE—THROUGH GLASS DOOR

UP AT Tom, glaring down at the donation-box display in the closed store. He looks a long moment, then, yes, he knows exactly what he's going to do. With a hard little smile and one more look at the display, he hurries away.

EXT. WATERFRONT STREET—TOM—NIGHT

TRUCK WITH him as he hurries down the street——accelerating his pace as the idea builds within him. He comes to a ***corner phone booth***, fishes out a dime, deposits the coin, starts dialing a number. The booth door remains open.

INT. CHARLIE'S ROOM—CLOSE—
TELEPHONE—NIGHT

RINGS loudly, on the night-stand beside the bed. PULL BACK to include Charlie, in bed, rumpled, groggily picking up the receiver.

CHARLIE (into phone)

Yeah, h'lo . . .? Who's this?

INTERCUT TO TOM IN PHONE BOOTH, as needed, during:

TOM (thickly)

Tom Desmond, Charlie. . . .

CHARLIE

You crazy, Tom? It's the middle of the night. Whattaya want?

TOM

My boat. I'm gonna get the money I owe you, Charlie, Tonight. And I want my boat.

CHARLIE

*Know something? You **are** crazy. You're——*

TOM

I'll bring the money, you bring the boat. I'll meet you at my slip in an hour.
  (hangs up)

CHARLIE

Wait a minute, Tom! You're——
  (exasperated)
Aaagh . . .!

He slams the receiver down disgustedly.

CUT TO:

INT. HOSPITAL ROOM—CLOSE—JULIE—NIGHT

asleep in the dimly-lighted room. PULL BACK SLOWLY to include her door——opening quietly. Tom leans into the room, calling softly:

> TOM
>
> *Julie . . .*

She stirs a bit, but doesn't awaken. (*NOTE:* She will have an IV taped to her arm in this scene.) Tom enters quietly, shuts the door. He's still joost a leetle bit dronk. He approaches the bed, leans down, kisses her lightly. Her eyes flutter open. She stares up at him, disoriented.

> JULIE (weakly)
>
> *Tom . . .?*
>   (he grins, nods)
> *It's——so late. What're you doing here . . .?*

> TOM
>
> *Jus' wanted to see you.*

She struggles to a half-sitting position, eyeing him curiously.

> JULIE
>
> *Something's wrong. I can smell it.*

> TOM (grins)
>
> *Tha's the booze. I been celebrating. Got a deal cooking down the coast . . . a chance to pick up a lot of bread . . .*

> JULIE (worried)
>
> *Down the coast? Where?*

> TOM
>
> *Well, I——um——I'll be traveling around for a while. It's a real good deal, Julie . . .*

> JULIE
>
> *I thought you had a job.*

ANGLE—FAVORING TOM

A bit startled. He'd forgotten about Willoughby. Then, remembering:

> TOM

Oh. Yeah. Well, you might as well know: I blew that one. And the boat's been repossessed. But I'm getting it out of hock tonight——

> JULIE

Tom—do you **have** *to leave town?*

> TOM

Baby, I'm not doing you—or Tina—any good around here . . .

> JULIE

Don't talk that way. Please.

> TOM

Well, it's true. I figured I'd try someplace else—change my luck. And this deal **came** *up . . . lot of money in it, Julie——*

ANGLE—FAVORING JULIE

> JULIE

It's something crooked, isn't it.

> TOM

Where'd you get that idea?

> JULIE

Tom, I don't want you to go . . .

> TOM

Now, Julie, there's nothing to get up-tight about. It's all settled . . .
   (prepares to flee)
Now go back to sleep. I'll call you every day—and I'll——

> JULIE (an entreaty)

Please, Tom——

> TOM

——send you the money as soon as I get it——

> JULIE

Tom—Wait—please——

> TOM

'Night, Julie. Gotta run. Got a million things to do . . .

He blows her a kiss, and hurries out of the room, trying not to hear:

JULIE (desperately)

Tom . . . ! !

But he's gone. Frantic now, beyond reason, Julie starts to climb out
of bed calling:

JULIE

Tom——!!

She's forgotten about the IV tube taped to her arm. As she struggles
out of bed, the tube pulls the IV standard over——it falls——the
bottle SMASHES on the floor——and Julie, weak, groggy——takes
a few steps and collapses. Seconds later, the door bursts open and
the NIGHT NURSE rushes in. An ORDERLY is behind her. The Nurse
hurries to Julie, who is unconscious on the floor.

NURSE

Call Doctor Gannon—hurry!

The Orderly runs out. The Nurse attends to Julie.

CUT TO:

INT. TOM'S APARTMENT—
TOWARD BEDROOM—NIGHT

Tom enters from the bedroom, carrying a suitcase. He pauses to
look around. The living room is littered with odds and ends of
marine equipment and reminders of Julie and Tina (baby toys,
wedding photos, clothes, etc.) He focuses on the marine equipment,
finds an old belaying pin. He picks it up, hefts it like a club. Then
there's a KNOCK at the door. Still holding the belaying pin, he
goes to open the door. Gannon greets him.

GANNON

Understand you're leaving, Tom. Just came by to wish you luck.

TOM (unconvinced)

Yeah, well, thanks. I'm pretty late. Gotta hurry . . .

GANNON (shuts the door)

*You didn't leave a forwarding address. If anything should happen
to Julie, we won't know where to find you.*

TOM (a beat, then)
She sent you here, didn't she.

ANGLE—FAVORING GANNON

GANNON (nods)
She's afraid you're about to get into trouble again.

TOM (without conviction)
She knows better than that.
    (then)
Anyway, this isn't your bag, Doc. It doesn't concern you at all.

GANNON (firmly)
*It concerns the welfare of my patient. And that, chum, is **my bag**.*

TOM
*Look—all I can give her is bad news. She'll be much better off without
me!*

GANNON
In other words, you're running out.

TOM
*Okay, so I'm running out! But I'm gonna get some money—a lot
of it—and I'm gonna see that she gets it all!*

GANNON
*Tom, if money's the big hang-up, I'll be happy to loan you whatever
you—*

TOM
There you go with your handouts again!

GANNON
A loan isn't a handout.

TOM
It is to me. I told you before, Doc: I don't want your lousy charity.

GANNON
You make it sound like a dirty word.

ANGLE—FAVORING TOM

TOM

It is. I grew up on it. My old man was on welfare. The checks weren't enough to support the family—so he had to sneak out and find a job.
   (then, bitterly)
Weird, huh? He had to hide the one thing he was proud of—so he could qualify for **charity**.
   (then)
And when they caught him, he lost everything. His welfare checks, his job—his pride, dignity, everything.

GANNON (touched)

Charity doesn't have to work that way.

TOM (bitterly)

Yeah, tell that to my old man.

GANNON (sharply)

I'm telling it to **you**. *What about* **your** *dignity—***your** *pride? You walk out on a sick wife and a 3-month-old baby—you reject anyone who tries to help—you destroy everything and everyone who really matters to you, including yourself! If that's "pride", Tom, you can have it. But don't expect anyone else to share it with you.*

TOM

I don't need anyone else!

GANNON

Not even Julie?
   (as Tom reacts)
She has her own kind of pride. It's built on **love**. *What's yours built on?*

A bristling moment. Then Tom grabs his suitcase, pushes past Gannon——and rushes out of the apartment, still holding the belaying pin. HOLD ON Gannon, at the door. He's done all he can. Is it enough?

CUT TO:

INT. CAFE—CLOSE—CASH REGISTER—NIGHT

RINGS up "NO SALE". PULL BACK to include the cashier, at

the open register, starting to count the day's receipts. The donation-box is still on the counter near the register. Now she looks up, a bit startled, as Tom bursts in. He carries his suitcase in one hand, the belaying pin in the other. He looks wild-eyed, desperate. The cashier shuts the cash register quickly, and:

> CASHIER
> *Sorry, mister, we're closed.*

ANGLE—FAVORING TOM

> TOM (nervously)
> *All I want is some coffee—and a piece of pie. Apple pie.*

She glances at the belaying pin, decides not to argue with him.

> CASHIER (hesitant)
> *I'll——see if there's any left.*

She exits, toward the kitchen. Tom is alone. He turns his attention to the donation-box display.

CLOSE SHOT—UP AT TOM

Sweating, fighting his own instincts, he lifts the belaying pin. But the action is halted in midair by the intrusion of:

> JULIE'S VOICE
> *Tom—Wait—please——*

He stiffens, tries again. But this time, he is halted by a jumble of overlapping voices, a PLAYBACK OF PREVIOUS DIALOGUE, hammering at his conscience:

> JULIE'S VOICE
> *It's something crooked, isn't it.*

> GANNON'S VOICE
> *She's afraid you're about to get in trouble again.*

> JULIE'S VOICE
> *Tom Desmond, you promised me you'd never get in trouble again . . .*

> GANNON'S VOICE
> *What about **your** pride, **your** dignity?*

JULIE'S VOICE
Tom——

GANNON'S VOICE
Tom——!!

It's more than Tom can bear. He drops the belaying pin——and runs out of the cafe.

ANGLE—THE CASHIER

Returning from the kitchen with some stale pie:

CASHIER
Apple's all gone. All we got is yesterday's rhubarb——

She stops. Tom, of course, is gone. With a shrug, she scrapes the stale pie into the sink.

EXT. HARBOR AREA—TRUCKING SHOT—NIGHT

Tom——running, running. Exhausted, drained of all emotion, he slows to a stop, drops his suitcase, sinks wearily to a sitting position on a coil of line. Alone on the deserted pier, he puts his face in his hands and weeps silently. Finally, the catharsis has run its course. As he tries to pull himself together:

CHARLIE'S VOICE (O.S.)
That you, Tom . . .?

Tom looks up——surprised, uncertain. Charlie looms out of the darkness.

CHARLIE (cont'd)
Been waiting for you, kid.

TOM (with difficulty)
Listen, Charlie—I——I——couldn't get the money. I——can't pay you.

CHARLIE
What're you talking about? The boat's all paid for.
   (Tom stares at him)
Tried to tell you on the phone. I got the check about 10 o'clock tonight.

                                     TOM
What check?

                                  CHARLIE
The one you sent me.
     (takes it from wallet)
*This one. Signed by a Doctor Joseph Cannon—or Gannon—something
like that . . .*

Tom grabs the check, takes it over to the light, stares at it in utter
disbelief.

CUT TO:

INT. WARD CORRIDOR—AT TELEPHONE BOOTH—WITH
TOM—DAY

Tom is just finishing a conversation on the telephone.

                              TOM (into phone)
*That's right—Tom Desmond. You can reach me at that dock number
most any time.*

ANGLE TOWARD ELEVATOR—DAY

as Gannon steps out, sees Tom at the phone, just as he hangs
up————he steps out of the booth.

                                     TOM
Oh, Doctor Gannon—I—I was on my way to see Julie.

                                  GANNON
I'm glad to see you changed your mind.

                                     TOM
About a lot of things.
     (nods toward phone)
*I was just talking to your people at the telethon. I told them I want
to help out. I know a lot of guys down at the dock. And—well . . .
I'm sure I can wring some money out of them, for the Clinic.*
     (pause)
Every penny counts, huh Doc?

GANNON (smiles, nods)
*I have a hunch the Clinic just acquired a great asset in you Tom.
Now why don't you go in and see Julie?*

Gannon starts off, Tom stops him.

TOM (sincerely)
*I—I—want to thank you for paying off my boat. That's—some kind
of a handout.*

GANNON
*A **loan** Tom—not a handout.*

TOM
I'll pay it back. Every cent. I swear I will.

GANNON
I don't have any doubt about it.

They start walking toward the Ward Desk——Tom stops for:

TOM
Hey—while my credit is still good—can I borrow another quarter?

Puzzled, Gannon takes a quarter from his pocket, hands it to Tom.
Then Gannon walks out through the double doors. PAN WITH
Tom to the Ward Desk, where he flips the coin in the air——then
deposits it in the donation-box display. Tom then heads down the
opposite corridor toward Julie's room as we:

FADE OUT.

THE END

A portion of a teleplay by Don Brinkley upon which a MEDICAL CENTER television series episode entitled "Countdown" was produced © Metro-Goldwyn-Mayer
Inc. MCMLXX.

INDEX